Super Cheap Fiji Travel Guide

"Once you visit Fiji, you'll understand why happiness is measured in smiles." - Unknown

Did you know you can fly on a private jet for $500? Yes, a fully private jet. Complete with flutes of champagne and reclinable creamy leather seats. Your average billionaire spends $20,000 on the exact same flight. You can get it for $500 when you book private jet empty leg flights.This is just one of thousands of ways you can travel luxuriously on a budget. You see there is a big difference between being cheap and frugal.

When our brain hears the word “budget” it hears deprivation, suffering, agony, even depression. But budget travel need not be synonymous with hostels and pack lunches. You can enjoy an incredible and luxurious trip to Fiji on a budget, just like you can enjoy a private jet flight for 10% of the normal cost when you know how.

Over 20 years of travel has taught me I could have a 20 cent experience that will stir my soul more than a $100 one. Of course, sometimes the reverse is true, my point is, spending money on travel is the best investment you can make but it doesn’t have to be at levels set by hotels and attractions with massive ad spends and influencers who are paid small fortunes to get you to buy into something you could have for a fraction of the cost.

This book is for those who love bargains and want to have the cold hard budget busting facts to hand (which is why we’ve included so many one page charts, which you can use as a quick reference), but otherwise, the book provides plenty of tips to help you shape your own Fiji experience.

We have designed these travel guides to give you a unique planning tool to experience an unforgettable trip without spending the ascribed tourist budget.

This guide focuses on Fiji’s unbelievable bargains. Of course, there is little value in traveling to Fiji and not experiencing everything it has to offer. Where possible, we’ve included super cheap workarounds or listed the experience in the Loved but Costly section.

When it comes to luxury budget travel, it’s all about what you know. You can have all the feels without most of the bills. A few days spent planning can save you thousands. Luckily, we’ve done the planning for you, so you can distill the information in minutes not days, leaving you to focus on what matters: immersing yourself in the sights, sounds and smells of Fiji, meeting awesome new people and feeling relaxed and happy.

This book reads like a good friend has travelled the length and breadth of Fiji and brought you back incredible insider tips.

So, grab a cup of tea or coffee, put your feet up and relax; you’re about to enter the world of enjoying Fiji on the Super Cheap. Oh, and don’t forget a biscuit. You need energy to plan a trip of a lifetime on a budget.

This travel guide is your step-by-step manual for unlocking luxury hotels, enjoying the best culinary offerings and once-in-a-lifetime luxury experiences in Fiji at a fraction of the usual cost.

Everyone's budget is different, but luxury is typically defined by first or business class seats on the airplane, five-star hotels, chauffeurs, exclusive experiences, and delectable fine dining. Yes, all of these can be enjoyed on a budget.

Finding luxury deals in Fiji simply requires a bit of research and planning, which this book has done for you. We have packed this book with local insider tips and knowledge to save you tens of thousands.

If the mere mention of the word luxury has you thinking things like "Money doesn't grow on trees," "I don't need anything fancy," "I don't deserve nice things," or "People who take luxury trips are shallow and materialistic/environmentally harmful/lack empathy, etc.," then stop. While we all know travel increases our happiness, research on the effects of luxury travel has proven even better results:

Reduced stress: A study published in the Journal of Travel Research found that individuals who visited luxury hotels reported feeling less stressed than those who in standard hotels.[1]

Increased happiness: A study conducted by the International Journal of Tourism Research found that luxury travel experiences lead to an increase in happiness and overall life satisfaction.[2] Researchers also found that luxury travel experiences can improve individuals' mental health by providing a sense of escape from daily stressors and enhancing feelings of relaxation and rejuvenation.

Enhanced creativity: Researchers found engaging in luxury travel experiences can stimulate creativity and lead to more innovative thinking.[3]

While all of this makes perfect sense; it feels much nicer to stay in a hotel room that's cleaned daily than in an Airbnb where you're cleaning up after yourself. What you might not know is that you can have all of that increased happiness and well-being without emptying your bank account. Does it sound too good to be true? This book will prove it isn't!

---

[1] Wöber, K. W., & Fuchs, M. (2016). The effects of hotel attributes on perceived value and satisfaction. Journal of Travel Research, 55(3), 306-318.

[2] Ladhari, R., Souiden, N., & Dufour, B. (2017). Luxury hotel customers' satisfaction and loyalty: An empirical study. International Journal of Hospitality Management, 63, 1-10.

[3] Kim, S., Kim, S. Y., & Lee, H. R. (2019). Luxury travel, inspiration, and creativity: A qualitative investigation. Tourism Management, 71, 354-366.

The Magical Power of Bargains

Have you ever felt the rush of getting a bargain? And then found good fortune just keeps following you?

Let me give you an example. In 2009, I graduated into the worst global recession for generations. One unemployed day, I saw a suit I knew I could get a job in. The suit was £250. Money I didn't have. Imagine my shock when the next day I saw the exact same suit (in my size) in the window of a second-hand shop (thrift store) for £18! I bought the suit and after three months of interviewing, without a single call back, within a week of owning that £18 suit, I was hired on a salary far above my expectations. That's the powerful psychological effect of getting an incredible deal. It builds a sense of excitement and happiness that literally creates miracles.

I have no doubt that the white powdery sands and magical rainforests of Fiji will uplift and inspire you but when you add the bargains from this book to your vacation, not only will you save a ton of money; you are guaranteed to enjoy a truly magical trip to Fiji.

Discover Fiji

With its palm-fringed beaches, turquoise waters, and warm hospitality, Fiji offers a unique blend of natural beauty, rich culture, and unforgettable experiences you won't find elsewhere. Approximately 56% of Fiji's land area is covered in forests. These forests are crucial for biodiversity conservation, and supporting local livelihoods. These forests also offer visitors a spectacular array of flora and fauna to discover.

Begin your journey by understanding Fiji's geography and climate. Comprising over 300 islands, Fiji is divided into two main groups: the larger Viti Levu and Vanua Levu, and the smaller outer islands. Each island offers its own unique charm, from the bustling capital of Suva to the secluded luxury resorts of the Mamanuca and

Yasawa Islands. Fiji enjoys a tropical maritime climate, with warm temperatures year-round and two distinct seasons: the wet season from November to April and the dry season from May to October. While the wet season brings occasional tropical storms, it also offers lush green landscapes and fewer crowds, making it an ideal time for super cheap hotel rates.

One of the highlights of visiting Fiji is experiencing its rich and vibrant culture. Fiji's history is as rich and colorful as its coral reefs. From ancient indigenous cultures to colonial influences, the islands have been shaped by the indigenous Fijian people, with their warm hospitality and deep-rooted customs. Today they welcome visitors with open arms, inviting them to partake in age-old ceremonies and rituals.

Even though the arrival of European explorers and settlers brought about significant changes, including the introduction of Christianity and the establishment of colonial rule, Fijian culture remained resilient, blending traditional practices with modern influences to create a unique identity.

Fiji's natural beauty is nothing short of breathtaking. Picture-perfect beaches stretch as far as the eye can see, fringed by swaying palm trees and lapped by crystal-clear waters. Beneath the waves, an underwater wonderland awaits, teeming with colorful coral gardens, tropical fish, and majestic marine creatures.

But Fiji's allure extends beyond its coastline. Inland, verdant rainforests cloak rugged mountains, hiding hidden waterfalls and ancient caves waiting to be explored. Hiking trails offer glimpses of rare flora and fauna.

Fiji operates on "Fiji Time," where schedules are more of a suggestion than a strict rule. The key to a great Fiji trip is to allow yourself to slow down, relax, and soak in the natural beauty surrounding you.

When you descend from the plane, you'll be greeted not just by the warm tropical breeze but also by the most infectious smiles you've ever seen. Seriously, Fijians are some of the friendliest folks on the planet! It's like they've got a special superpower for making you feel instantly at home, whether you're arriving solo or with a group of pals.

And let's not forget the food! Oh, the food. From fresh seafood straight off the boat to tropical fruits so juicy they'll make your taste buds sing, Fiji's culinary scene is a feast for the senses. And don't even get me started on the traditional Fijian lovo – a mouthwatering feast cooked in an underground oven that'll have you licking your lips for days.

While Fiji is often associated with luxury, it's entirely possible to experience the islands' splendor without breaking the bank. On average, a tourist might spend $200 USD per day, inclusive of accommodation, meals, transportation, and activities but we will show you in the next 200 pages how to spend from as little as $20 a day and have the time of your life!

Weird and wonderful facts about Fiji

- **Fiji Time**: In Fiji, there's a concept known as "Fiji Time." This isn't just a casual attitude—it's a way of life. Things tend to happen at a slower pace, and schedules are often more flexible than in other parts of the world. It's a reminder to visitors to relax and enjoy the moment rather than rushing through experiences.
- **Kava Ceremony**: Kava, a traditional Fijian drink made from the root of the pepper plant, holds significant cultural importance. Participating in a kava ceremony is a unique experience where visitors can join locals in drinking this mildly intoxicating beverage. It's a symbol of friendship and hospitality in Fijian culture.
- **No Snakes**: Fiji is one of the few places in the world where you won't find any native land snakes. Due to its isolation and strict biosecurity measures, the islands have remained free from these reptiles. This fact often surprises visitors, especially those from regions where snakes are common.
- **Underwater Post Office**: Fiji is home to the world's first and only underwater post office, located off the coast of Vanua Levu. Visitors can snorkel or dive to the post office, where they can purchase waterproof postcards and mail them to friends and family with a unique underwater postmark.
- **Cannibalism History**: While it may sound macabre, cannibalism was practiced in Fiji in ancient times. Tribes would engage in warfare, and defeated enemies would sometimes be consumed as a way of asserting dominance and absorbing their strength. However, this practice ceased with the arrival of European missionaries and colonial rule.
- **Fiji Banded Iguana**: Found only in Fiji, the Fiji banded iguana is a fascinating reptile known for its striking blue and green coloration. It's one of the world's most endangered iguanas, with efforts underway to protect its habitat and promote conservation awareness.
- **Fiji Mermaid**: In the late 19th and early 20th centuries, sideshows and traveling exhibitions often featured "Fiji mermaids," purported to be mythical creatures from the islands. In reality, these were usually fabricated specimens created by stitching together the upper body of a monkey or ape with the tail of a fish.
- **Beqa Fire Walking**: Beqa Island is famous for its traditional fire-walking ceremony, known as "vilavilairevo." Participants, known as "vilavilairevo warriors," walk across scorching hot stones without experiencing burns. This ancient ritual is believed to be a demonstration of spiritual power and strength.
- **Taveuni Island's International Date Line**: Taveuni Island is unique in that it straddles the International Date Line, allowing visitors to stand with one foot in today and the other in tomorrow. It's a fun and quirky experience to celebrate New Year's Eve twice by simply crossing a small stretch of land.
- **Fiji's Heart-shaped Islands**: Fiji is home to several heart-shaped islands, such as Tavarua and Matangi Island. These naturally formed islands have become popular symbols of romance and love, attracting honeymooners and couples seeking a romantic getaway.

Know before you go

- **Health Precautions**: Fiji is a tropical destination, so it's essential to take health precautions before your visit. Consider getting vaccinated for diseases such as hepatitis A and typhoid and ensure your routine vaccinations are up to date. Mosquito-borne illnesses like dengue fever and Zika virus can be a concern, so use insect repellent. In Fiji, citronella oil is particularly effective in warding off mosquitoes. Mix it with moisturizer for optimal coverage during your stay.
- **Currency and Payments**: The currency used in Fiji is the Fijian dollar (FJD). While credit cards are widely accepted in major tourist areas and resorts, it's advisable to carry some cash for smaller establishments and markets. ATMs are available in cities and towns, but they may be less common in rural areas and depending on your provider they carry fees.
- **Sim Card:** You can purchase a Vodafone SIM card for around $10 USD, depending on the package you choose, offering data, local calls, and international calling options. These SIM cards are readily available at Vodafone stores, as well as at the Nadi and Suva international airports upon arrival.
- **Transportation**: Fiji is made up of over 300 islands, so transportation between islands can vary. Domestic flights, ferries, and water taxis are common modes of transport. Plan your inter-island travel in advance, especially during peak seasons, and be prepared for potential delays due to weather or other factors.
- **Respect for Culture**: Fijians are known for their warmth and hospitality, so it's important to respect their culture and customs. When visiting villages or participating in traditional ceremonies, dress modestly and follow local protocols. Always ask for permission before taking photographs, especially of people.
- **Weather and Climate**: The dry season, from May to October, is considered the best time to visit, with lower humidity and less rainfall. However, even during the wet season, from November to April, you can still enjoy sunny days interspersed with brief showers.
- **Water Safety**: While Fiji's waters are inviting, it's essential to practice water safety, especially if you're not a confident swimmer. Pay attention to warning signs and currents, and swim only in designated safe areas. If engaging in water sports like snorkeling or diving, ensure you use reputable operators with proper safety equipment.
- **Environmental Conservation**: Fiji's natural beauty is one of its biggest attractions, so it's crucial to minimize your environmental impact during your visit. Avoid single-use plastics, such as bottles and bags, and support eco-friendly initiatives and businesses that prioritize sustainability.
- **Language**: English is the official language of Fiji and is widely spoken, especially in tourist areas. However, Fijian and Hindi are also commonly spoken by locals. Learning a few basic Fijian phrases, such as "bula" (hello) and "vinaka" (thank you), can go a long way in connecting with locals.

What to Pack

Packing smart can help you save money during your trip to Fiji while ensuring you have all the essentials for a fantastic experience. Here's what you should consider packing:

- **Reusable Water Bottle**: Fiji's tap water is generally safe to drink, so bring a reusable water bottle to stay hydrated and avoid purchasing bottled water, which can be costly and environmentally unfriendly.
- **Sun Protection**: Fiji's tropical climate means plenty of sun, so pack sunscreen, sunglasses, and a wide-brimmed hat to protect yourself from harmful UV rays. Bringing these items from home can save you money compared to buying them at tourist shops or resorts.
- **Snorkeling Gear**: Pack a travel snorkel. Renting snorkeling gear at resorts or tour operators can add up quickly, so bringing your own equipment can save you money and ensure a better fit and quality.
- **Lightweight Clothing**: Pack lightweight, breathable clothing suitable for warm weather, including swimsuits, shorts, T-shirts, and lightweight pants or dresses. Quick-drying fabrics are ideal for beach activities and water sports.
- **Insect Repellent**: Packing insect repellent (citronella and lemongrass are more effective than DEET in Fiji) can help protect you from bug bites and potential illnesses, saving you from having to purchase it locally.
- **Waterproof Bag or Dry Bag**: Keep your belongings dry while enjoying water activities by packing a waterproof bag or dry bag. This can also double as a beach bag to carry essentials like sunscreen, a towel, and a water bottle.
- **First Aid Kit**: Pack a basic first aid kit with essentials like bandages, antiseptic wipes, pain relievers, and any prescription medications you may need. This can save you from having to purchase these items at higher prices in tourist areas.
- **Reusable Tote Bag**: Bring a reusable tote bag for shopping or carrying items during your travels. Many stores in Fiji charge for plastic bags, so having your own tote bag can help you save money and reduce plastic waste.
- **Travel Adapter**: Fiji uses Type I electrical outlets, so if you're bringing electronic devices, make sure to pack a suitable travel adapter to charge your devices without having to purchase one locally.

Some of Fiji's Best Bargains

Free Village Visits

Fiji's villages boast a rich cultural tapestry deeply rooted in tradition. Historically, these villages were organized around chiefly systems, with close-knit communities governed by chiefs and elders. Traditional Fijian architecture, characterized by bures (thatched huts), still dots the landscape alongside modern structures. Village life revolves around communal activities like meke (traditional dances), yaqona (kava) ceremonies, and feasting, fostering strong bonds among villagers. Subsistence agriculture, fishing, and craftsmanship are integral to their way of life, providing sustenance and income. Despite modernization, many villages maintain a strong connection to their cultural heritage, preserving customs and rituals passed down through generations.

Some Fijian villages extend a warm invitation to visitors eager to immerse themselves in the traditional way of life, all without charging a dime. Here are a couple of villages renowned for their free hospitality:

- **Navala Village**: Tucked away in the highlands of Viti Levu, Navala is famous for its picturesque setting and well-preserved traditional Fijian architecture. Visitors are welcomed with open arms, invited to explore the village and learn about daily life, customs, and traditions. You might have the chance to participate in a kava ceremony, witness traditional dances, or even join in on community activities.
- **Nukubalavu Village**: Located on the stunning island of Vanua Levu, Nukubalavu offers visitors a rare glimpse into authentic Fijian village life. Here, you can stroll through lush tropical gardens, visit local homes, and engage in cultural activities like weaving and wood carving. The villagers are incredibly welcoming, eager to share their heritage and traditions with visitors from near and far.

Stay in Bure's

These are traditional Fijian bungalows which offer a rustic charm that whispers of timeless tradition and laid-back luxury.

Imagine waking up to the sound of waves lapping against the shore, sunlight filtering through the woven walls, and the soft caress of a tropical breeze. Step onto the wooden veranda, adorned with handcrafted furniture and swaying hammocks, and feel your worries melt away as you soak in the breathtaking vistas of white sand beaches and crystal-clear waters stretching to the horizon and when staying in Fijian Bure's, you can have this experience for as little as $30!

You'll find budget-friendly bures in popular Fiji destinations like Nadi, Denarau Island, Coral Coast, and the Yasawa Islands.

Natural Hot Springs

Nestled amidst the verdant landscapes of Fiji, Sabeto Hot Springs is a haven for relaxation seekers. These thermal pools boast mineral-rich waters believed to have healing properties, making them a popular destination for locals and tourists alike. Surrounded by lush tropical foliage, the setting is nothing short of idyllic, offering a serene escape from the hustle and bustle of everyday life.

What's even better is that entry to Sabeto Hot Springs is just $9. t's the perfect opportunity to unwind, recharge, and connect with the natural beauty of Fiji without having to worry about breaking the bank.

Beachfront Accommodations

Finding affordable beachfront accommodations in Fiji is entirely possible, allowing you to wake up to the soothing sounds of the ocean without breaking the bank.

- **Dorm rooms in resorts:** Dormitory-style accommodations within resorts in Fiji work similarly to hostel dormitories, offering budget-friendly options for travelers looking to share a room with others to save money. These dorms often feature bunk beds or single beds arranged in shared rooms, along with communal facilities such as bathrooms, common areas, and sometimes shared kitchens. They are available to cater to budget-conscious travelers, backpackers, and those seeking a social atmosphere where they can meet fellow travelers but they are set within expensive resorts! $5 sleep in a $500 a night resort anyone?
- **Hostels and Backpacker Resorts**: Fiji boasts several budget-friendly hostels and backpacker resorts that offer beachfront accommodations. Prices can start from as low as $20 to $30 per night for dormitory beds, while private rooms may range from $50 to $80 per night.
- **Guesthouses and Bed & Breakfasts**: These accommodations often provide cozy rooms with basic amenities and a more personalized touch. Prices can vary depending on the location and level of comfort, but you can generally find options starting from $50 to $100 per night.
- **Airbnb Rentals**: Prices can vary widely depending on the size, location, and amenities of the rental. However, budget-conscious travelers can often find beachfront accommodations starting from $50 to $100 per night for a private room or $100 to $200 per night for an entire home.

Free Coconut Husking and Weaving Demonstrations

Some resorts and cultural centers offer complimentary demonstrations of traditional Fijian crafts such as coconut husking and weaving. Watch skilled artisans create intricate designs using natural materials and learn about the cultural significance of these ancient crafts.

The Pacific Harbour Arts Village is a cultural hub located on the Coral Coast of Viti Levu. Here, visitors can immerse themselves in Fijian culture through various activities, including traditional coconut craft demonstrations.

Cheap Spa Treatments

Fiji's spa treatments trace back to ancient practices rooted in natural healing. Influenced by indigenous Fijian traditions, these therapies often incorporate local ingredients like coconut, papaya, and native herbs renowned for their rejuvenating properties.

Forget expensive resort treatments, head to Indulge at local wellness center. Prices for massages typically start from $30-$50 for an hour-long session, while facials and other pampering services range from $20-$40, providing affordable relaxation!

- Senikai Spa & Wellness Retreat (Nadi, Viti Levu): Situated in the heart of Nadi, Senikai Spa & Wellness Retreat offers a tranquil oasis for relaxation and rejuvenation. With a focus on holistic wellness, the center provides a variety of spa treatments, including massages, facials, and body scrubs, using natural and locally-sourced ingredients. The serene ambiance and attentive staff make it a favorite among locals and tourists alike.
- Koro Sun Resort & Rainforest Spa (Savusavu, Vanua Levu): Nestled amidst lush rainforest surroundings in Savusavu, Koro Sun Resort & Rainforest Spa offers an idyllic setting for wellness retreats. Guests can indulge in a range of spa treatments inspired by Fijian traditions, such as coconut exfoliation, banana leaf wraps, and hot stone massages. The resort's holistic approach to wellness, combined with its stunning natural beauty, makes it a top choice for those seeking relaxation and renewal.

Markets

Step into a Fijian market, and you'll find yourself immersed in a sensory symphony. The air is alive with the intoxicating scent of ripe tropical fruits, mingling with the spicy aroma of freshly ground spices. Stalls overflow with a kaleidoscope of colors, as vendors proudly display their wares – plump papayas, golden pineapples, ruby-red tomatoes, and emerald-green spinach. Each fruit and vegetable is a testament to Fiji's fertile soil and abundant sunshine, nurtured by the hands of generations of farmers.

Located in the heart of Fiji's capital city, Suva Municipal Market stands as one of the largest and most vibrant markets in the country, teeming with activity from dawn till dusk. Here, amidst the bustling crowds and vibrant stalls, visitors can peruse a vast array of fresh produce, tropical fruits, and aromatic spices sourced from across the islands. From plump papayas and fragrant pineapples to crisp taro and creamy coconuts, the market's bounty reflects Fiji's fertile lands and diverse agricultural heritage.

In addition to fresh produce, Suva Municipal Market is a treasure trove of Fijian handicrafts, textiles, and souvenirs, with vendors showcasing their skills in weaving, carving, and pottery. Visitors can browse intricately woven mats, hand-carved wooden artifacts, and vibrant saris, each item telling a story of tradition and craftsmanship passed down through generations.

Haggling Tips: Approach vendors with a friendly demeanor and a willingness to engage in conversation. Start by asking for the price and then politely negotiate for a lower rate, keeping in mind that haggling is a common practice in Fijian markets. Be respectful and patient, and don't be afraid to walk away if the price isn't right.

Enjoy Local Beer and Spirits

Fijian beers boast a crisp, clean taste that perfectly complements the tropical climate. And the best part? You won't have to break the bank to indulge in a bottle of this liquid gold. With prices ranging from $3 to $5 per bottle, it's an affordable way to quench your thirst while immersing yourself in the laid-back vibes of Fiji.

But perhaps you're craving something with a bit more kick—a spirit that packs a punch and leaves you feeling warm from the inside out. Enter Fijian rum, a beloved local favorite that's as smooth as it is flavorful. Made from sugarcane grown in the fertile soils of Fiji, this amber nectar boasts notes of caramel, spice, and a hint of tropical sweetness. And while it may sound like a luxury indulgence, you'll be pleasantly surprised to find that a bottle of Fijian rum won't cost you an arm and a leg. With prices ranging from $15 to $25 per bottle, it's an economical choice for those looking to elevate their island experience without breaking the bank.

Public Transportation

Utilize cost-effective public transportation options like buses, minibusses, and shared taxis to navigate Fiji's main islands. Fares are incredibly affordable, with bus tickets starting from $1 depending on the distance traveled, enabling you to traverse different regions economically.

BBQ's with free live music

Enjoying a barbecue with live music is a fantastic way to experience the vibrant culture and laid-back atmosphere of Fiji. Here are some of the best places in Fiji where you can indulge in a delicious BBQ feast accompanied by free live music:

- **Port Denarau, Nadi**: Port Denarau is a bustling marina complex in Nadi, Fiji, known for its lively atmosphere and waterfront dining options. Several restaurants and bars along the marina offer BBQ dinners with live music performances, providing a perfect setting to enjoy delicious food while overlooking the boats and ocean.
- **Musket Cove Island Resort, Malolo Lailai Island**: Musket Cove Island Resort is located on Malolo Lailai Island in the Mamanuca Islands chain. The resort hosts regular beachfront BBQ nights featuring live music and traditional Fijian entertainment. Guests can savor grilled seafood, meats, and local specialties while enjoying the stunning sunset views.
- **Coco Palms, Pacific Harbour**: Coco Palms is a popular beachside restaurant and bar located in Pacific Harbour, known as the "Adventure Capital of Fiji." The establishment hosts weekly BBQ nights with live music performances, offering a relaxed ambiance and mouthwatering grilled dishes paired with refreshing cocktails.
- **Volivoli Beach Resort, Rakiraki**: Volivoli Beach Resort is situated in Rakiraki on the northern coast of Viti Levu. The resort organizes regular beachside BBQs accompanied by live music, allowing guests to dine under the stars while listening to local musicians perform traditional Fijian tunes.
- **Cloud 9 Floating Bar, Mamanuca Islands**: Cloud 9 is a unique floating platform located in the Mamanuca Islands, offering stunning views of the surrounding turquoise waters. The venue hosts BBQ parties with live DJ sets and occasional live music performances, creating a lively atmosphere for guests to enjoy delicious food and drinks.

Diving and snorkeling experiences in Fiji

Fiji;s coral reefs burst with kaleidoscopic life. Snorkel amid vibrant fish, dancing through an underwater tapestry. Glide alongside gentle giants like manta rays, their graceful movements mesmerizing. But the real thrill? Encountering sharks, rulers of the deep and diving doesn't have to take a bite out of your bank balance!

- **Mana Island**: Mana Island, located in the Mamanuca Islands chain, offers budget-friendly diving and snorkeling opportunities. The island is surrounded by vibrant coral reefs teeming with marine life, including colorful fish, turtles, and reef sharks. There are lot of budget accommodations are available on the island, making it an ideal destination for budget-conscious divers and snorkelers.
- **Beqa Lagoon**: Beqa Lagoon, off the southern coast of Viti Levu, is renowned for its spectacular diving sites, including the famous Beqa Shark Dive and there are tours from $80.
- **Yasawa Islands**: The Yasawa Islands chain offers budget-friendly diving and snorkeling experiences, with numerous dive sites accessible from budget accommodations on the islands.
- **Taveuni**: Taveuni, known as the "Garden Island" of Fiji, offers budget-friendly diving and snorkeling experiences in the Somosomo Strait. The strait is home to world-class dive sites, including the Great White Wall and Rainbow Reef, where colorful coral formations and abundant marine life await. Budget accommodations are available on Taveuni, making it an affordable destination for underwater enthusiasts.
- **Kadavu**: Kadavu, located south of Viti Levu, offers budget-friendly diving and snorkeling experiences in the Great Astrolabe Reef. The reef is one of the largest in the world and is home to a diverse array of marine life, including manta rays, sharks, and colorful coral gardens.

Island Hopping Pass

If you plan to do a lot of island hopping, the Bula Pass (expensive, as it is) is ideal for island hopping, granting access to multiple islands with ease.

The Bula Pass is a flexible ferry ticket that allows travelers to hop on and off vessels operated by Awesome Adventures Fiji within the Yasawa Islands group.

The pass is available for a range of durations, typically ranging from 5 to 15 days, offering travelers the flexibility to choose the length of their island-hopping adventure.

The Bula Pass grants access to numerous islands within the Yasawa group, including popular destinations like Nacula, Nanuya, Naviti, Waya, and Drawaqa, among others. Each island offers unique experiences, from pristine beaches and crystal-clear waters to cultural activities and hiking opportunities.

The Bula Pass can be purchased online through the Awesome Adventures Fiji website or at designated sales outlets in Fiji. It's advisable to book in advance, especially during peak travel seasons, to secure preferred travel dates and accommodations.

The cost of the Bula Pass varies depending on the duration selected, ranging from approximately $200 to $600 FJD per person for a 5 to 15-day pass. Prices may also vary depending on any promotional offers or discounts available at the time of booking. If you plan to buy it google “Bula Pass Discount Code” to get an additional code for a discount.

Government subsided activities

In Fiji, the government subsidizes various cultural and recreational activities to promote tourism and preserve the country's rich heritage and you can benefit from this!

- **Cultural Shows and Festivals**: The Fijian government often sponsors cultural shows, festivals, and events that showcase traditional Fijian music, dance, and cuisine. These events provide visitors with an opportunity to experience authentic Fijian culture and entertainment at a minimal cost. Keep an eye out for events such as the Hibiscus Festival, Fiji Day celebrations, and cultural performances held at community centers or public venues.
- **Arts and Crafts Workshops**: Government-funded arts and crafts workshops are occasionally organized to promote traditional Fijian craftsmanship and cultural preservation. Visitors can participate in hands-on workshops where they can learn to weave mats, carve wooden artifacts, or create traditional Fijian jewelry under the guidance of local artisans.
- **Heritage Trails and Guided Tours**: The Fijian government supports initiatives aimed at preserving the country's historical sites and natural landmarks. Heritage trails and guided tours led by trained guides are often subsidized to encourage visitors to explore Fiji's rich history and biodiversity. Tourists can embark on guided hikes through lush rainforests, visit ancient archaeological sites, and learn about Fiji's colonial heritage through subsidized tours organized by government agencies. To book heritage trails and guided tours in Fiji, including those subsidized by the government, you can reach out to the Fiji Tourism Board. Here's how you can contact them:

Fiji Tourism Board

- Website: Fiji Tourism
- Email: info@tourismfiji.com.fj

- Phone: +679 672 2433

How to Enjoy ALLOCATING Money in Fiji

'Money's greatest intrinsic value—and this can't be overstated—is its ability to give you control over your time.' - Morgan Housel

Notice I have titled the chapter how to enjoy allocating money in Fiji. I'll use saving and allocating interchangeably in the book, but since most people associate saving to feel like a turtleneck, that's too tight, I've chosen to use wealth language. Rich people don't save. They allocate. What's the difference? Saving can feel like something you don't want or wish to do and allocating has your personal will attached to it.

And on that note, it would be helpful if you considered removing the following words and phrase from your vocabulary for planning and enjoying your Fiji trip:

- Wish
- Want
- Maybe someday

These words are part of poverty language. Language is a dominant source of creation. Use it to your advantage. You don't have to wish, want or say maybe someday to Fiji. You can enjoy the same things millionaires enjoy in Fiji without the huge spend.

'People don't like to be sold-but they love to buy.' - Jeffrey Gitomer.

Every good salesperson who understands the quote above places obstacles in the way of their clients' buying. Companies create waiting lists, restaurants pay people to queue outside in order to create demand. People reason if something is so in demand, it must be worth having but that's often just marketing. Take this sales maxim 'People don't like to be sold-but they love to buy and flip it on its head to allocate your money in Fiji on things YOU desire. You love to spend and hate to be sold. That means when something comes your way, it's not 'I can't afford it,' it's 'I don't want it' or maybe 'I don't want it right now'.

Saving money doesn't mean never buying a latte, never taking a taxi, never taking vacations (of course, you bought this book). Only you get to decide on how you spend and on what. Not an advice columnist who thinks you can buy a house if you never eat avocado toast again.

I love what Kate Northrup says about affording something: "If you really wanted it you would figure out a way to get it. If it were that VALUABLE to you, you would make it happen."

I believe if you master the art of allocating money to bargains, it can feel even better than spending it! Bold claim, I know. But here's the truth: Money gives you freedom and options. The more you keep in your account and or invested the more freedom and options you'll have. The principal reason you should save and allocate money is TO BE FREE! Remember, a trip's main purpose is relaxation, rest and enjoyment, aka to feel free.

When you talk to most people about saving money on vacation. They grimace. How awful they proclaim not to go wild on your vacation. If you can't get into a ton of debt enjoying your once-in-a-lifetime vacation, when can you?

When you spend money 'theres's a sudden rush of dopamine which vanishes once the transaction is complete. What happens in the brain when you save money? It increases feelings of security and peace. You don't need to stress life's uncertainties. And having a greater sense of peace can actually help you save more money.' Stressed out people make impulsive financial choices, calm people don't.'

The secret to enjoying saving money on vacation is very simple: never save money from a position of lack. Don't think 'I wish I could afford that'. Choose not to be marketed to. Choose not to consume at a price others set. Don't save money from the flawed premise you don't have enough. Don't waste your time living in the box that society has created, which says saving money on vacation means sacrifice. It doesn't.

Traveling to Fiji can be an expensive endeavor if you don't approach it with a plan, but you have this book which is packed with tips. The biggest other asset is your perspective.

Winning the Vacation Game

The inspiration for these books struck me during a Vipassana meditation retreat. As I contemplated the excitement that precedes a vacation, I couldn't help but wish that we could all carry that same sense of anticipation in our daily lives. It was from this introspection that the concept of indulging in luxurious trips on a budget was born. The driving force behind this idea has always been the prevalence of disregarded inequalities.

A report from the Pew Charitable Trusts unveiled a stark reality: only about 4% of individuals born into the lowest income quintile, the bottom 20%, in the United States manage to ascend to the top income quintile during their lifetime. This trend is mirrored in many parts of Europe, underscoring the immense hurdles faced by those from disadvantaged backgrounds, including myself, in their pursuit of financial security.

To compound this, a comprehensive study conducted by researchers at Stanford University and published in the Journal of Personality and Social Psychology illuminated a compelling connection between career choices, personal fulfillment, and income. It revealed that individuals who prioritize intrinsic factors like passion often find themselves with lower average incomes, highlighting the intricate dynamics at play in the pursuit of one's dreams. Either you're in a low-income career, believing you can't afford to travel, or you're earning well but desperately need a vacation due to your work being mediocre at best. Personally, I believe it's better to do what you love and take time to plan a luxury trip on a budget. Of course, that, in itself, is a luxurious choice not all of us have. I haven't even mentioned Income, education, and systemic inequalities that can lock restrict travel opportunities for many.

Despite these challenging realities, I firmly believe that every individual can have their dream getaway. I am committed to providing practical insights and strategies that empower individuals to turn their dream vacations into a tangible reality without breaking the bank.

How to use this book

Google and TripAdvisor are your on-the-go guides while traveling, a travel guide adds the most value during the planning phase, and if you're without Wi-Fi. Always download the google map for your destination - having an offline map will make using this guide much more comfortable. For ease of use, we've set the book out the way you travel, booking your flights, arriving, how to get around, then on to the money-saving tips. The tips we ordered according to when you need to know the tip to save money, so free tours and combination tickets feature first. We prioritized the rest of the tips by how much money you can save and then by how likely it was that you could find the tip with a google search. Meaning those we think you could find alone are nearer the bottom. I hope you find this layout useful. If you have any ideas about making Super Cheap Insider Guides easier to use, please email me philgattang@gmail.com

A quick note on How We Source Super Cheap Tips
We focus entirely on finding the best bargains. We give each of our collaborators $2,000 to hunt down never-before-seen deals. The type you either only know if you're local or by on the ground research. We spend zero on marketing and a little on designing an excellent cover. We do this yearly, which means we just keep finding more amazing ways for you to have the same experience for less.

Now let's get started with juicing the most pleasure from your trip to Fiji with the least possible money!

Planning your trip

Fiji experiences a tropical climate with two main seasons: the wet season and the dry season.

The wet season typically runs from November to April. During this time, temperatures are high, humidity levels rise, and rainfall is more frequent, often in the form of heavy downpours and occasional tropical storms. Despite the rain, this season is characterized by lush vegetation and vibrant landscapes.

Conversely, the dry season spans from May to October. During this period, temperatures are slightly cooler, humidity levels drop, and rainfall diminishes significantly. Days are generally sunny and pleasant, making it an ideal time for outdoor activities such as diving, snorkeling, and hiking.

Regardless of the season, Fiji maintains a warm climate year-round, with temperatures averaging around 25-30°C (77-86°F). Visitors can enjoy the islands' beauty and activities throughout the year, with each season offering its own unique charm and opportunities for exploration.

Plan your trip outside of Australian and New Zealand school holidays

Timing your trip strategically can yield significant savings. Accommodation prices tend to rise during school holidays in Australia and New Zealand, as most tourists originate from these countries.

Australian and New Zealand school holidays vary depending on the state or territory. However, they generally follow similar patterns:

Australian School Holidays:

- Term 1: Generally late January to early April
- Term 2: Generally late April to late June
- Term 3: Generally mid-July to late September
- Term 4: Generally mid-October to mid-December

New Zealand School Holidays:

- Term 1: Generally early February to mid-April
- Term 2: Generally late April to early July
- Term 3: Generally mid-July to late September
- Term 4: Generally mid-October to mid-December

Peak season, from June to August and around Christmas, also sees increased prices. Budget-friendly trips often coincide with Fiji's cyclone season from November to April, offering more affordable rates despite occasional rainstorms.

Think about island hopping

Each island visit in Fiji not only consumes time but also money. Once you leave Viti Levu, you'll need either a boat transfer or a flight to reach the next island. If you're set on exploring multiple islands, focus on the Mamanuca and Yasawa Islands, and consider staying on islands accessible via the Yasawa Flyer – a high-speed catamaran offering convenient hop-on-hop-off passes, though at quite an expense. A cheaper alternative is to book accomodation with free transfers between different islands in Mamanuca and Yasawa Islands.

Opt for public buses

Most Fijians travel around Viti Levu and Vanua Levu, the two largest islands, via public buses. These buses are budget-friendly, with fares starting at approximately FJD$1 per journey. Longer trips cost around FJD$4. While these buses may lack air conditioning and make frequent stops, for longer journeys, consider booking with Sunbeam or Pacific Buses, which offer air-conditioned rides with guaranteed seating. Taxis start at FJD$2 and typically charge around FJD$15 for a 15-minute ride.

Utilize transportation included in day trip excursions

Many tour companies on Viti Levu provide complimentary transportation within a certain radius from their departure point, saving you money on taxi fares. Take advantage of this service if you need transport between different locations, such as from your resort to a restaurant.

Negotiate multi-day discounts with tour companies

Some travel agencies in Fiji offer various tours, such as South Sea Cruises, which organizes trips to private island day clubs, snorkeling tours, and more. Booking a second tour during your trip can often save you up to 20%. Additionally, many tour, scuba, and cruise companies offer repeat visitor discounts, so it's worth inquiring about potential savings.

Choose ferry travel over domestic flights

Traveling to islands like Ovalau, Vanua Levu, and Taveuni via ferry is typically much cheaper than flying domestically, often costing around 10% of a flight ticket. This option is ideal if you have flexibility in your schedule, as ferry timetables can be subject to delays due to weather conditions. Remember to pack snacks and dress comfortably for the journey.

Local Markets contain Gold

Fiji's markets abound with fresh fruits and vegetables sold in generous portions, offering better value than imported produce typically found in grocery stores. Markets also feature handmade souvenirs, spices, snacks, and kava at significantly lower prices than retail stores.

Activate a local SIM card for internet access

Mobile data is relatively inexpensive in Fiji compared to many other destinations. Major cell phone networks like Digicel and Vodafone often run promotions for tourists at the airport, offering free or discounted data plans. Expect to pay around FJD$10 for 20 GB of data, valid for two weeks at standard rates. While some hotels offer free internet access, outer island accommodations may charge around FJD$20 per day with usage limits. Compare coverage maps of different providers to ensure connectivity throughout your trip, or simply disconnect and embrace the island lifestyle fully.

Bring your own snorkeling gear

Bringing your own snorkeling equipment ensures you can enjoy this activity at any time and on any island without rental shop constraints. While some resorts provide snorkeling gear as part of the stay, others charge up to FJD$20 per day for rental.

Save on accommodation, splurge on activities

Fiji's reputation for being an expensive destination holds true. To maximize value, consider budget-friendly accommodations and allocate your budget toward day trips and activities. Private island resorts can cost thousands per night, with additional expenses for meals and transport. Staying in a hostel or hotel on Viti Levu and venturing out on day trips to private island beach clubs or resorts can offer more value for your money. Most day tours last eight hours, providing a full day of luxury and adventure.

Opt for local beverages or bring your own alcohol

Fiji boasts locally produced coconut rum, gin, and beer, offering affordable options for island indulgence. Imported spirits and wines incur hefty charges at bars due to high taxes. Duty-free shops at airports offer the best deals on alcohol, allowing each adult passenger to bring up to 2.25 liters of spirits or 4.5 liters of wine and beer.

Remember, cash is King in Fiji

International credit cards often incur additional charges of 2 to 5% on purchases throughout Fiji. ATM withdrawals typically involve high conversion fees.

Free Festivals

In Fiji, several festivals and events take place throughout the year, offering you the opportunity to experience the rich culture, traditions, and celebrations of the Fijian people. While many festivals may have nominal fees for certain activities or attractions, there are also several free festivals and events that travelers can enjoy. Here's a month-by-month guide to some of the free festivals and events in Fiji, along with their dates and locations:

January:

- *Fiji Showcase Festival*: Held annually in Suva, the Fiji Showcase Festival celebrates Fijian culture, arts, and entertainment. Visitors can enjoy traditional dance performances, music, food stalls, and artisan markets. (Location: Suva, Viti Levu)

February:

- *Holi Festival*: Also known as the Festival of Colors, Holi is celebrated by the Indian community in Fiji with vibrant colors, music, and dancing. Visitors can join in the festivities and participate in color throwing activities. (Locations: Various cities and towns with large Indian communities)

March:

- *Fiji Day*: Celebrated on March 7th, Fiji Day commemorates the country's independence from British colonial rule. Festivities include cultural performances, parades, and traditional ceremonies. (Locations: Nationwide)

April:

- *Bula Festival*: Held in Nadi, the Bula Festival celebrates Fijian hospitality and culture with a week-long program of events, including parades, concerts, food stalls, and beauty pageants. (Location: Nadi, Viti Levu)

May:

- *Fiji International Jazz and Blues Festival*: This annual music festival features performances by local and international jazz and blues artists. Visitors can enjoy live music concerts, workshops, and jam sessions. (Location: Various venues, Suva)

June:

- *Fiji Music Festival*: Organized by the Fiji Performing Rights Association, the Fiji Music Festival showcases the talents of local musicians and bands with live performances across various genres of music. (Locations: Nationwide)

July:

- *Fiji Hibiscus Festival*: The Fiji Hibiscus Festival is a week-long event held in Suva, featuring beauty pageants, cultural performances, carnival rides, food stalls, and live entertainment. (Location: Suva, Viti Levu)

August:

- *Bula Festival*: Another Bula Festival is held annually in August in Nadi, featuring similar festivities to the April event, including parades, concerts, and cultural displays. (Location: Nadi, Viti Levu)

September:

- *Savusavu Festival*: Held in the town of Savusavu on Vanua Levu, the Savusavu Festival celebrates the local community with cultural performances, sports competitions, food stalls, and traditional ceremonies. (Location: Savusavu, Vanua Levu)

October:

- *Diwali Festival*: Celebrated by the Indian community in Fiji, Diwali is the Festival of Lights and is marked by the lighting of lamps, fireworks, and traditional prayers. Visitors can witness colorful decorations and participate in cultural activities. (Locations: Various cities and towns with large Indian communities)

November:

- *Fiji Day*: On November 3rd, Fiji celebrates its national independence with parades, cultural performances, and traditional ceremonies. Visitors can join in the festivities and experience the patriotic spirit of the Fijian people. (Locations: Nationwide)

December:

- *Christmas Festivities*: Throughout December, Fijians celebrate Christmas with religious services, carol singing, community gatherings, and festive decorations. Visitors can experience the joyous atmosphere and participate in holiday events. (Locations: Nationwide)

When to go to each Fiji island

- **Viti Levu**: As the main island and home to Nadi International Airport, Viti Levu offers a range of accommodations and activities year-round. The dry season, from May to October, is the most popular time to visit, offering sunny days, lower humidity, and minimal rainfall. However, you may find better deals on accommodations during the shoulder seasons of April and November, when the weather is still pleasant, and tourist crowds are thinner.
- **Vanua Levu**: Fiji's second-largest island, Vanua Levu, experiences similar weather patterns to Viti Levu. The dry season (May to October) is ideal for visiting, with comfortable temperatures and less rainfall. Look for deals on accommodations during the shoulder seasons, particularly in April and November, to enjoy quieter beaches and cheaper rates.
- **Taveuni**: Known as the "Garden Island" of Fiji, Taveuni boasts lush rainforests, waterfalls, and abundant marine life. The dry season (May to October) offers excellent weather for outdoor activities such as hiking, diving, and snorkeling. For cheaper deals and fewer tourists, consider visiting during the shoulder seasons of April and November when accommodations may offer discounts.
- **Yasawa Islands**: The Yasawa Islands are renowned for their stunning beaches, crystal-clear waters, and vibrant coral reefs. The dry season (May to October) is the most popular time to visit, offering sunny days and ideal conditions for water sports and beach activities. For budget-friendly deals, consider visiting during the shoulder seasons of April and November, when accommodation rates may be lower, and the islands are less crowded.
- **Mamanuca Islands**: Close to Viti Levu and easily accessible from Nadi, the Mamanuca Islands are famous for their picture-perfect beaches and luxury resorts. The dry season (May to October) is peak tourist season, with higher prices and more crowds. To snag cheaper deals, consider visiting during the shoulder seasons of April and November, when accommodation rates may be more affordable, and you can still enjoy pleasant weather.
- **Kadavu**: Kadavu is a remote and unspoiled island known for its pristine reefs and diverse marine life. The dry season (May to October) offers the best weather for diving, snorkeling, and exploring the island's natural beauty. For budget-conscious travelers, consider visiting during the shoulder seasons of April and November when accommodation rates may be lower, and you can still enjoy favorable weather conditions.

Which Island?

Fiji comprises over 330 islands, each offering unique experiences for travelers. Here's a comprehensive overview of some of the main Fiji islands, along with their pros and cons for travelers, including information on how to get there, the cost of accommodation, and popular attractions:

- **Viti Levu**:
    - Home to Nadi International Airport, making it easily accessible for international travelers.
    - Offers a wide range of accommodations, from budget guesthouses to luxury resorts.
    - Diverse attractions, including coral reefs, waterfalls, and cultural sites like the Sri Siva Subramaniya Temple.
    - Touristy areas can be crowded, especially around Nadi and Denarau Island.
    - Some beaches may be affected by industrial development or pollution.
  - How to Get There: Most international flights land at Nadi International Airport on Viti Levu.
  - Cost of Accommodation: Accommodation prices vary depending on location and quality, ranging from budget options starting at around $30 USD per night to luxury resorts costing several hundred dollars per night.
  - Popular Attractions: Sigatoka Sand Dunes National Park, Sabeto Hot Springs, Coral Coast, and Navua River.

- **Vanua Levu**:
    - Offers a more laid-back atmosphere compared to Viti Levu, with fewer tourists.
    - Rich cultural experiences, including traditional Fijian villages and markets.
    - Excellent diving and snorkeling spots, such as the Great Sea Reef and Namena Marine Reserve.
    - Limited direct international flights; most visitors arrive via domestic flights from Nadi or Suva.
    - Accommodation options may be more limited compared to Viti Levu, with fewer luxury resorts.
  - How to Get There: Domestic flights from Nadi or Suva to Labasa Airport or Savusavu Airport on Vanua Levu.
  - Cost of Accommodation: Accommodation ranges from budget guesthouses starting at around $20 USD per night to mid-range resorts costing $100-$200 USD per night.
  - Popular Attractions: Savusavu Bay, Labasa Market, Rainbow Reef, and Taveuni Island.

- **Taveuni**:
    - Known as the "Garden Island" for its lush rainforests, waterfalls, and diverse wildlife.
    - Excellent hiking opportunities, including the Lavena Coastal Walk and Bouma National Heritage Park.

        - World-class diving and snorkeling sites, such as the Rainbow Reef and Great White Wall.
        - Limited direct international flights; most visitors arrive via domestic flights from Nadi or Suva.
        - Accommodation options may be limited compared to larger islands like Viti Levu.
    - How to Get There: Domestic flights from Nadi or Suva to Matei Airport on Taveuni.
    - Cost of Accommodation: Accommodation options range from budget guesthouses starting at around $30 USD per night to eco-resorts costing $200-$300 USD per night.
    - Popular Attractions: Tavoro Waterfalls, Lake Tagimaucia, Vuna Blowholes, and Waitavala Natural Waterslide.

- **Yasawa Islands**:
        - Stunning white-sand beaches, crystal-clear waters, and vibrant coral reefs.
        - Remote and unspoiled natural beauty, offering a peaceful and relaxing atmosphere.
        - Opportunities for snorkeling, kayaking, and cultural experiences with local villages.
        - Cons:
        - Limited accommodation options; primarily boutique resorts and budget backpacker accommodations.
        - Limited amenities and services on some islands; visitors may need to bring supplies.
    - How to Get There: Yasawa Flyer ferry service or seaplane flights from Nadi or Denarau Island.
    - Cost of Accommodation: Accommodation options range from budget backpacker resorts starting at around $40 USD per night to luxury private island resorts costing $500+ USD per night.
    - Popular Attractions: Sawa-i-Lau Caves, Blue Lagoon, Mantaray Island, and Waya Island.

- **Mamanuca Islands**:
        - Close proximity to Nadi and Denarau Island, making them easily accessible for day trips or short getaways.
        - Stunning beaches, clear waters, and excellent diving and snorkeling opportunities.
        - Wide range of accommodation options, including family-friendly resorts and luxury private island retreats.
        - Can be crowded during peak tourist season, especially around popular resorts and day-trip destinations.
        - Prices may be higher compared to more remote islands due to popularity and demand.
    - How to Get There: Yasawa Flyer ferry service or private boat charters from Nadi or Denarau Island.
    - Cost of Accommodation: Accommodation options range from budget beachfront resorts starting at around $100 USD per night to luxury overwater bungalows costing $1000+ USD per night.
    - Popular Attractions: Cloud 9 floating bar, Monuriki Island (where Cast Away was filmed), Manta Ray Island, and Mana Island.

- **Kadavu**:
    - Pros:
    - Remote and off-the-beaten-path destination, offering pristine beaches and untouched natural beauty.
    - Excellent diving and snorkeling opportunities, including the Great Astrolabe Reef.
    - Authentic Fijian cultural experiences with local villages and communities.
    - Cons:
    - Limited transportation options; most visitors arrive via domestic flights from Nadi or Suva.
    - Accommodation options may be limited compared to more developed islands.
  - How to Get There: Domestic flights from Nadi or Suva to Kadavu Airport.
  - Cost of Accommodation: Accommodation options range from budget guesthouses starting at around $50 USD per night to eco-resorts costing $300+ USD per night.
  - Popular Attractions: Great Astrolabe Reef, Mount Washington, Kadavu Kula Eco Park, and Namuana Village.

Best small islands

There are several options that offer affordable accommodations, activities, and a more intimate experience. Here are some of the best tiny islands for budget travelers in Fiji:

- **Beqa Island**: Beqa Island is located off the southern coast of Viti Levu and offers budget-friendly accommodations, including guesthouses and backpacker lodges. Visitors can explore the island's rugged coastline, hike through lush rainforests, and enjoy snorkeling and diving at nearby reefs, such as Beqa Lagoon.
- **Nacula Island (Yasawa Islands)**: Nacula Island is part of the Yasawa Islands chain and is known for its stunning beaches and budget-friendly accommodations. Backpacker resorts and guesthouses offer affordable options for travelers, while the island's pristine waters are perfect for snorkeling, kayaking, and beachcombing.
- **Naviti Island (Yasawa Islands)**: Naviti Island is another budget-friendly option in the Yasawa Islands, offering backpacker accommodations and budget resorts. Travelers can explore the island's rugged coastline, hike to viewpoints for stunning vistas, and relax on secluded beaches without the crowds found on larger islands.
- **Beachcomber Island**: Beachcomber Island is a tiny, uninhabited island located in the Mamanuca Islands chain. While accommodation options are limited to a single budget-friendly resort, the island offers a lively atmosphere with beach parties, water sports, and social activities, making it a popular choice for budget travelers looking for a fun and affordable getaway.
- **Mantaray Island (Yasawa Islands)**: Mantaray Island is a budget-friendly destination known for its stunning coral reefs and laid-back atmosphere. Backpacker resorts and budget accommodations cater to travelers on a budget, while activities such as snorkeling, diving, and hiking are available at affordable prices.

- **Wayalailai Island (Yasawa Islands)**: Wayalailai Island offers budget-friendly accommodations in the Yasawa Islands chain, with backpacker lodges and guesthouses providing affordable options for travelers. Visitors can explore the island's lush interior, hike to viewpoints for panoramic vistas, and relax on pristine beaches without the crowds.
- **Matamanoa Island**: Matamanoa Island is a small, privately-owned island located in the Mamanuca Islands chain. While it offers luxury accommodations, budget travelers can opt for more affordable beachfront bures or backpacker dormitories. The island's stunning beaches, crystal-clear waters, and laid-back atmosphere make it a budget-friendly paradise.

Cheapest Method of getting to each island

While it's true that sticking to just a couple of islands can help save money on transportation and accommodation, island hopping in Fiji can be surprisingly affordable if you plan smartly.

Firstly, consider the location of the islands you want to visit. Some islands, like those in the Mamanuca group, are closer to the main island of Viti Levu and are therefore cheaper and easier to reach. Opting for these islands can save you both time and money on transportation.

Additionally, look out for free transfers that come with accomodation or discount ferry deals. Many tour operators offer bundled deals for island hopping, which can include transportation, accommodation, and even activities, making it a cost-effective option.

Here is the cheapest method of getting to each island:

Island	Pros	Cons	Cheapest Method of Getting There
Mamanuca Islands	- Close to Nadi	- Can be crowded with tourists	Ferry
Yasawa Islands	- Less crowded, more remote	- Limited accommodation and facilities	Ferry
Taveuni	- Known as the "Garden Island" with lush scenery	- More challenging to reach	Domestic flights or ferry
Vanua Levu	- Quieter and less touristy than Viti Levu	- Limited tourist infrastructure, fewer amenities	Domestic flights or ferry
Kadavu	- Pristine diving and snorkeling spots	- Remote location with limited transportation options	Domestic flights or ferry
Beqa Island	- Famous for shark diving	- Limited accommodation and activities	Ferry
Ovalau	- Historical sites and colonial charm	- Limited tourist facilities, quieter atmosphere	Ferry

To secure discounts on Fiji ferries, consider the following tips:

- **Book in Advance**: Many ferry companies offer discounted rates for travelers who book tickets well in advance of their departure date. Look for early booking deals on the ferry company's website or through authorized agents. This can save you $100 on getting to the Yasawa group of islands.
- **Travel Off-Peak**: Traveling during off-peak seasons or on weekdays can often result in lower fares compared to peak travel times or weekends when demand is higher. Check the ferry company's schedule for off-peak times and take advantage of discounted rates.

Here are the URLs for some of the major ferry services operating in Fiji:

- **Awesome Adventures Fiji**:
  - Website: https://www.awesomefiji.com/
- **South Sea Cruises**:
  - Website: https://www.ssc.com.fj/
- **Tiger IV Ferries** (Taveuni and Vanua Levu):
  - Website: https://www.tiger4ferry.com/
- **Yasawa Flyer**:
  - Website: https://www.yasawa.com/
- **Goundar Shipping**:
  - Website: https://www.goundarshipping.com/

Booking Flights

How to Find Heavily Discounted Private Jet Flights to or from Fiji

If you're dreaming of travelling to Fiji on a private jet you can accomplish your dream for a 10th of the cost.

Empty leg flights, also known as empty leg charters or deadhead flights, are flights operated by private jet companies that do not have any passengers on board. These flights occur when a private jet is chartered for a one-way trip, but the jet needs to return to its base or another location without passengers.

Rather than flying empty, private jet companies may offer these empty leg flights for a reduced price to travelers who are flexible and able to fly on short notice. Because the flight is already scheduled and paid for by the original charter, private jet companies are willing to offer these flights at a discounted rate in order to recoup some of the cost.

Empty leg flights can be a cost-effective way to experience the luxury and convenience of private jet travel.

There are several websites that offer empty leg flights for booking. Here are a few:

JetSuiteX: This website offers discounted, last-minute flights on private jets, including empty leg flights.

PrivateFly: This website allows you to search for empty leg flights by location or date. You can also request a quote for a custom flight if you have specific needs.

Victor: This website offers a variety of private jet services, including empty leg flights.

Sky500: This website offers a variety of private jet services, including empty leg flights.

Air Charter Service: This website allows you to search for empty leg flights by location or date. You can also request a quote for a custom flight if you have specific needs.

Keep in mind that empty leg flights are often available at short notice, so it's a good idea to be flexible with your travel plans if you're looking for a deal. It's also important to do your research and read reviews before booking a flight with any company.

RECAP: To book an empty leg flight in Fiji, follow these steps:

1. Research and identify private jet companies and or brokers that offer empty leg flights departing from Fiji. You can use the websites mentioned earlier, such as JetSuiteX, PrivateFly, Victor, Sky500, or Air Charter Service, to search for available flights.

2. Check the availability and pricing of empty leg flights that match your travel dates and destination. Empty leg flights are often available at short notice.

3. Contact the private jet company or broker to inquire about booking the empty leg flight. Be sure to provide your travel details, including your preferred departure and arrival times, number of passengers, and any special requests.

4. Confirm your booking and make payment. Private jet companies and brokers typically require full payment upfront, so be prepared to pay for the flight in advance.

5. Arrive at the airport at least 30 minutes before the scheduled departure time.

6. Check in at the private jet terminal and go through any necessary security checks. Unlike commercial airlines, there is typically no long queue or security checks for private jet flights.

7. Board the private jet and settle into your seat. You will have plenty of space to stretch out and relax, as well as access to amenities such as Wi-Fi, entertainment systems, and refreshments.

How to Find CHEAP FIRST-CLASS Flights to Fiji

Upgrade at the airport

Airlines are extremely reluctant to advertise price drops in first or business class tickets so the best way to secure them is actually at the airport when airlines have no choice but to decrease prices dramatically because otherwise they lose money. Ask about upgrading to business or first-class when you check-in. If you check-in online look around the airport for your airlines branded bidding system.

Use Air-miles

When it comes to accruing air-miles for American citizens **Chase Sapphire Reserve card** ranks top. If you put everything on there and pay it off immediately you will end up getting free flights all the time, aside from taxes.

Get 2-3 chase cards with sign up bonuses, you'll have 200k points in no time and can book with points on multiple airlines when transferring your points to them.

Please note, this is only applicable to those living in the USA. In the Bonus Section we have detailed the best air-mile credit cards for those living in other countries.

How many miles does it take to fly first class?
New York City to Fiji could require anywhere from 70,000 to 120,000 frequent flyer miles, depending on the airline and the time of year you plan to travel.

How to Fly Business Class to Fiji cheaply

Fiji Airways is a popular airline that operates flights from Los Angeles to Fiji with the cheapest business class options. In low season this route typically started at around $1,000-$1,500 per person for a round-trip ticket.

The average cost for a round-trip flight from New York City to Fiji typically ranged from around $400 to $1200 for an economy seat, so if travelling business class is important to you, Fiji Airways is likely to be the best bang for your buck.

To find the best deals on business class flights to Fiji, follow these steps:

1. Use travel search engines: Start by searching for flights on popular travel search engines like Google Flights, Kayak, or Skyscanner. These sites allow you to compare prices from different airlines and book the cheapest available business option.
2. Sign up for airline newsletters: Airlines often send out exclusive deals and promotions to their email subscribers. Sign up for TAP Air Portugal's newsletter to receive notifications about special offers and discounts on business class flights.
3. Book in advance: Booking your flight well in advance can help you secure a better deal on business class tickets. Aim to book your flight at least two to three months before your travel date.

Cheapest route to Fiji from America

At the time of writing Fiji Airways Lingus are flying to Fiji Nadi, direct for around $340 each way.

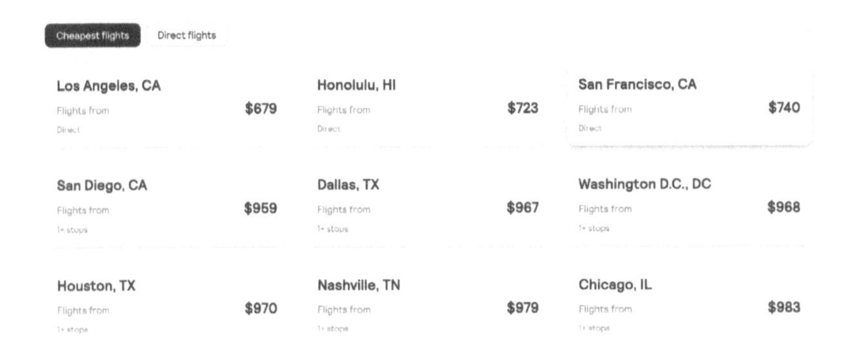

The prices above are return flight prices.

Cheapest Flight Route From Australia

Finally, one experience that's cheap for Australian travellers - flights to Fiji! You can fly direct with JetStar for under $300 return from multiple airports!

Select departure location

Cheapest flights | Direct flights

Melbourne Flights from $300 Direct	**Sydney** Flights from $306 Direct	**Brisbane** Flights from $311 Direct
Canberra Flights from $371 Direct	**Adelaide** Flights from $391 Direct	**Gold Coast** Flights from $424 1+ stops
Hobart Flights from $482 1+ stops	**Townsville** Flights from $483 1+ stops	**Cairns** Flights from $519 1+ stops

Cheapest Flight Route From New Zealand

Fiji Airways and Air New Zealand are both flying direct to Nadi from $376 return.

Cheapest Flight Route From Europe

The average cost of a flight from Europe to Fiji can vary widely depending on factors such as the time of booking, seasonality, airline, route, and class of travel. Generally, flights from Europe to Fiji can range from around €800 to €1500 return. The key to getting the cheaper ticket is flying from one of the major flight hubs with Fiji Airways. If they don't have any flights for your dates, you can break the trip down into two parts.

1. Start in London and fly to LAX with Norwegian Air Shuttle - a low-cost carrier known for offering budget-friendly fares on transatlantic routes, including flights between London Gatwick (LGW) and Los Angeles International Airport (LAX).

2. Fly from LAX with Fiji Airways to Nadi, Fiji.

The cheapest flight hubs to fly from in Europe to Fiji are these four:

- **London**: With several major airports like Heathrow (LHR), Gatwick (LGW), and Stansted (STN), London is a common departure point for flights to Fiji.
- **Paris**: Charles de Gaulle Airport (CDG)
- **Amsterdam**: Amsterdam Airport Schiphol (AMS)
- **Frankfurt**: Frankfurt Airport (FRA) is one of the busiest airports in Europe and a major hub for international flights to Fiji.

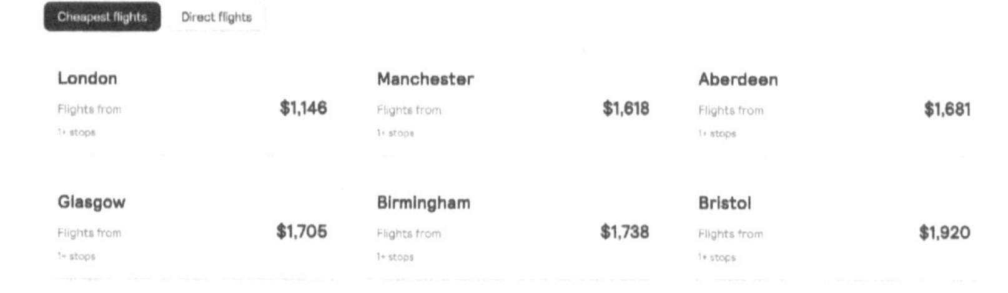

London comes in around $400 cheaper than the other departing flight hubs depending on dates. The airline is Fiji Airways and the route is London Heathrow to Los Angeles (LAX) and then onto Nadi, Fiji.

How to Find Super Cheap Flights to Fiji

Luck is just an illusion. Anyone can find incredible flight deals. If you can be flexible you can save huge amounts of money. In fact, the biggest tip I can give you for finding incredible flight deals is simple: find a flexible job. Don't despair if you can't do that theres still a lot you can do.

Book your flight to Fiji on a Tuesday or Wednesday

Tuesdays and Wednesdays are the cheapest days of the week to fly. You can take a flight to Fiji on a Tuesday or Wednesday for less than half the price you'd pay on a Thursday Friday, Saturday, Sunday or Monday.

Start with Google Flights (but NEVER book through them)

I conduct upwards of 50 flight searches a day for readers. I use google flights first when looking for flights. I put specific departure but broad destination (e.g Europe) and usually find amazing deals.

The great thing about Google Flights is you can search by class. You can pick a specific destination and it will tell you which time is cheapest in which class. Or you can put in dates and you can see which area is cheapest to travel to.

But be aware Google flights does not show the cheapest prices among the flight search engines but it does offer several advantages

1. You can see the cheapest dates for the next 8 weeks. Other search engines will blackout over 70% of the prices.
2. You can put in multiple airports to fly from. Just use a common to separate in the from input.
3. If you're flexible on where you're going Google flights can show you the cheapest destinations.
4. You can set-up price tracking, where Google will email you when prices rise or decline.

Once you have established the cheapest dates to fly go over to skyscanner.net and put those dates in. You will find sky scanner offers the cheapest flights.

Get Alerts when Prices to Fiji are Lowest

Google also has a nice feature which allows you to set up an alert to email you when prices to your destination are at their lowest. So if you don't have fixed dates this feature can save you a fortune.

Baggage add-ons

It may be cheaper and more convenient to send your luggage separately with a service like sendmybag.com Often the luggage sending fee is cheaper than what the airlines charge to check baggage. Visit Lugless.com or luggagefree.com in addition to sendmybag.com for a quotation.

Loading times

Anyone who has attempted to find a cheap flight will know the pain of excruciating long loading times. If you encounter this issue use google flights to find the cheapest dates and then go to skyscanner.net for the lowest price.

Always try to book direct with the airline

Once you have found the cheapest flight go direct to the airlines booking page. This is advantageous in the current covid cancellation climate, because if you need to change your flights or arrange a refund, its much easier to do so, than via a third party booking agent.

That said, sometimes the third party bookers offer cheaper deals than the airline, so you need to make the decision based on how likely you think it is that disruption will impede you making those flights.

More flight tricks and tips

www.secretflying.com/usa-deals offers a range of deals from the USA and other countries. For example you can pick-up a round trip flight non-stop from from the east coast to johannesburg for $350 return on this site

Scott's cheap flights, you can select your home airport and get emails on deals but you pay for an annual subscription. A free workaround is to download Hopper and set search alerts for trips/price drops.

Premium service of Scott's cheap flights.
They sometime have discounted business and first class but in my experience they are few and far between.

JGOOT.com has 5 times as many choices as Scott's cheap flights.

kiwi.com allows you to be able to do radius searches so you can find cheaper flights to general areas.

Finding Error Fares

Travel Pirates (www.travelpirates.com) is a gold-mine for finding error deals. Subscribe to their newsletter. I recently found a reader an airfare from Montreal-Brazil for a $200 round trip (mistake fare!). Of course these error fares are always certain dates, but if you can be flexible you can save a lot of money.

Things you can do that might reduce the fare to Fiji:--

- Use a VPN (if the booker knows you booked one-way, the return fare will go up)
- Buy your ticket in a different currency

If all else fails...

If you can't find a cheap flight for your dates I can find one for you. I do not charge for this nor do I send affiliate links. I'll send you a screenshot of the best options I find as airlines attach cookies to flight links. To use this free service please review this guide and send me a screenshot of your review - with your flight hacking request. I aim to reply to you within 12 hours. If it's an urgent request mark the email URGENT in the subject line and I will endeavour to reply ASAP.

How to Find CHEAP FIRST-CLASS Flights to Fiji

Upgrade at the airport
Airlines are extremely reluctant to advertise price drops in first or business class tickets so the best way to secure them is actually at the airport when airlines have no choice but to decrease prices dramatically because otherwise they lose money. Ask about upgrading to business or first-class when you check-in. If you check-in online look around the airport for your airlines branded bidding system. KLM have terminals where you can bid on upgrades.

Use Air-miles

When it comes to accruing air-miles for American citizens **Chase Sapphire Reserve card** ranks top. If you put everything on there and pay it off immediately you will end up getting free flights all the time, aside from taxes.

Get 2-3 chase cards with sign up bonuses, you'll have 200k points in no time and can book with points on multiple airlines when transferring your points to them.

Please note, this is only applicable to those living in the USA. In the Bonus Section we have detailed the best air-mile credit cards for those living in the UK, Canada, Germany, Austria, Fiji and Australia.

Accommodation

Your two biggest expenses when travelling to Fiji are accommodation and food. This section is intended to help you cut these costs dramatically without compromising on those luxury feels:

How to Book a Five-star Hotel consistently on the Cheap in Fiji

The cheapest four and five-star hotel deals are available when you 'blind book'. Blind booking is a type of discounted hotel booking where the guest doesn't know the name of the hotel until after they've booked and paid for the reservation. This allows hotels to offer lower prices without damaging their brand image or cannibalizing their full-price bookings.

Here are some of the best platforms for blind booking a hotel in Fiji:

Hotels.com - Where Every Stay Counts:

Hotels.com is your go-to mate when it comes to scoring sweet deals on luxury accommodations in Fiji. With its "Reward Nights" program offering a free night's stay for every ten nights booked, you'll feel like you've hit the jackpot in no time. Plus, Hotels.com often features "Secret Prices" on select properties, so you can unlock even more savings on your island getaway. Whether you're craving a beachfront villa or a secluded resort retreat, Hotels.com has got you covered.

Agoda - Your Gateway to Exclusive Deals:

For savvy travelers looking to snag a luxury hotel in Fiji for less, Agoda is the ultimate treasure trove of exclusive deals and discounts. With its extensive network of hotel partners and insider pricing, Agoda offers unbeatable rates on top-notch accommodations that will make you feel like royalty without blowing your budget. Plus, its easy-to-use website and mobile app make booking a breeze, so you can spend less time searching and more time soaking up the sun on Fiji's stunning beaches.

Travelocity - Your Fairy Godmother of Travel:

If you're dreaming of a luxurious escape to Fiji but don't want to break the bank, Travelocity is here to make your wishes come true. With its "Price Match Guarantee" ensuring that you'll get the best price on your accommodations, you can book with confidence knowing that you're getting the most bang for your buck. Plus, Travelocity's "Top Secret Hotels" feature offers exclusive deals on luxury properties that are too good to pass up. So, why wait? Dive into Travelocity's treasure trove of savings and start planning your ultimate getaway to Fiji today!

Dorm rooms within resorts

Dorm rooms within resorts offer affordable options with access to amenities like swimming pools and breakfast buffets. Finding the best dorm rooms within resorts in Fiji with starting prices can vary depending on the season, location, and resort. However, here are a few popular options:

Smugglers Cove Beach Resort & Hotel (Nadi):
Starting prices for dorm rooms: Around FJD 30 per night (approximately $15 USD).
This resort offers budget-friendly dormitory accommodation with access to amenities like a swimming pool, beach, and breakfast buffet.
Bamboo Backpackers (Nadi):
Starting prices for dorm rooms: Around FJD 25 per night (approximately $12.50 USD).
Known for its laid-back atmosphere, this hostel provides affordable dormitory accommodation with basic facilities.
Aquarius On The Beach (Nadi):
Starting prices for dorm rooms: Around FJD 40 per night (approximately $20 USD).
This beachfront hostel offers dormitory rooms with sea views and access to a restaurant, bar, and outdoor pool.
Beachcomber Island Resort (Mamanuca Islands):
Starting prices for dorm rooms: Around FJD 90 per night (approximately $45 USD).
Located on a private island, this resort offers dormitory accommodation with access to various water sports activities and entertainment.
South Sea Island Resort (Mamanuca Islands):
Starting prices for dorm rooms: Around FJD 80 per night (approximately $40 USD).
This resort provides dormitory accommodation on a small island with access to snorkeling, kayaking, and cultural activities.

Cheapest Liveaboard experiences

Imagine waking each dawn to the sun's gentle caress, painting the horizon in hues of amber and gold, as you sip your morning brew amidst the tranquil expanse of the sea. This is possible with live-aboard diving. Here are the cheapest options:

- **Fiji Siren**:
  - Fiji Siren offers budget-friendly liveaboard diving experiences in Fiji. Prices can vary depending on the length of the trip and the itinerary, but they often offer competitive rates compared to other operators.
- **Nai'a Liveaboard**:
  - Nai'a Liveaboard offers various diving itineraries in Fiji, including trips to popular dive sites like the Bligh Waters and the Somosomo Strait. While not the cheapest option, they do offer occasional discounts and specials, particularly during off-peak seasons.
- **Fiji Aggressor**:
  - Fiji Aggressor operates liveaboard dive cruises to explore the reefs and marine life of Fiji. They sometimes offer promotions or last-minute deals, which can make their trips more affordable.
- **Island Dancer II**:
  - Island Dancer II offers liveaboard diving adventures in Fiji, focusing on exploring the underwater treasures of the region. They may have special offers or discounted rates available for certain departure dates.

Where to stay if you want to walk to attractions on each island

If you're looking to stay within walking distance of major attractions on each major island in Fiji, here are some recommendations:

Viti Levu:

- *Suva*: In Suva, the capital city of Fiji located on Viti Levu, you'll find various accommodations within walking distance of major attractions such as the Suva Municipal Market, Fiji Museum, and Thurston Gardens. Look for hotels or guesthouses in the downtown area or along Victoria Parade for convenient access to these sites.

Vanua Levu:

- *Labasa*: Labasa is the largest town on Vanua Levu and offers accommodations within walking distance of local attractions such as Subrail Park, the Labasa Market, and Sangam Temple. Look for hotels or guesthouses in the town center for easy access to these sites.

Taveuni:

- *Waiyevo*: Waiyevo is a small town on Taveuni island and serves as a hub for exploring the island's natural attractions, including Tavoro Waterfalls and Lavena Coastal Walk. Look for accommodations in or near Waiyevo for easy access to these hiking trails and other attractions.

Yasawa Islands:

- *Nacula Island*: Nacula Island is one of the Yasawa Islands known for its stunning beaches and coral reefs. While accommodations are limited on the island, there are a few resorts and budget-friendly options within walking distance of attractions such as Blue Lagoon Beach and Sawa-i-Lau Caves.

Mamanuca Islands:

- *Beachcomber Island*: Beachcomber Island is a popular destination in the Mamanuca Islands known for its white sandy beaches and vibrant marine life. Accommodations on the island are primarily resort-style, with options available within walking distance of attractions such as Barefoot Island Resort and snorkeling spots.

Kadavu Island:

- *Vunisea*: Vunisea is the main town on Kadavu Island and offers accommodations within walking distance of local attractions such as Vunisea Lookout and nearby beaches. Look for guesthouses or eco-resorts in the town center for convenient access to these sites.

Cheapest all-inclusive hotels

Picture yourself lounging on powdery white sands, caressed by gentle ocean breezes, as attentive staff cater to your every whim...Here are some of the cheapest all-inclusive hotels in Fiji with starting prices:

- **Mango Bay Resort**:
  - Location: Coral Coast, Viti Levu
  - Starting Price: Approximately $150 USD per night (all-inclusive)
  - Features: Mango Bay Resort offers budget-friendly all-inclusive packages that include meals, non-alcoholic beverages, and select activities such as kayaking, snorkeling, and village tours.
- **Uprising Beach Resort**:
  - Location: Pacific Harbour, Viti Levu
  - Starting Price: Approximately $200 USD per night (all-inclusive)
  - Features: Uprising Beach Resort offers all-inclusive packages that include meals, non-alcoholic beverages, and select activities such as paddleboarding, snorkeling, and cultural performances.
- **Club Fiji Resort**:
  - Location: Nadi, Viti Levu
  - Starting Price: Approximately $250 USD per night (all-inclusive)
  - Features: Club Fiji Resort offers affordable all-inclusive packages that cover meals, non-alcoholic beverages, and select activities such as kayaking, paddleboarding, and beach volleyball.
- **Fiji Hideaway Resort & Spa**:
  - Location: Coral Coast, Viti Levu
  - Starting Price: Approximately $300 USD per night (all-inclusive)
  - Features: Fiji Hideaway Resort & Spa offers all-inclusive packages that include meals, non-alcoholic beverages, and select activities such as snorkeling, kayaking, and Fijian cultural experiences.
- **Barefoot Kuata Island**:
  - Location: Kuata Island, Yasawa Islands
  - Starting Price: Approximately $200 USD per night (all-inclusive)
  - Features: Barefoot Kuata Island offers budget-friendly all-inclusive packages that cover meals, non-alcoholic beverages, and select activities such as snorkeling, kayaking, and guided hikes.
- **Beachcomber Island Resort**:
  - Location: Beachcomber Island, Mamanuca Islands
  - Starting Price: Approximately $250 USD per night (all-inclusive)
  - Features: Beachcomber Island Resort offers all-inclusive packages that include meals, non-alcoholic beverages, and select activities such as snorkeling, kayaking, and beach volleyball.

Cheapest Hotel Chains:

- **Travellers Beach Resort**:
- Location: Nadi, Viti Levu
- Starting Price: Approximately $30 - $50 USD per night
- **Nomads Skylodge**:
- Location: Nadi, Viti Levu
- Starting Price: Approximately $30 - $50 USD per night
- **Beach Escape Villas**:
- Location: Nadi, Viti Levu
- Starting Price: Approximately $40 - $60 USD per night

Cheapest Four-Star Hotels:

- **Tanoa International Hotel**:
- Location: Nadi, Viti Levu
- Starting Price: Approximately $100 - $150 USD per night
- **Tokatoka Resort Hotel**:
- Location: Nadi, Viti Levu
- Starting Price: Approximately $100 - $150 USD per night
- **Mercure Nadi**:
- Location: Nadi, Viti Levu
- Starting Price: Approximately $100 - $150 USD per night

Best Boutique Hotels :

- **Fiji Beachouse**:
- Location: Coral Coast, Viti Levu
- Starting Price: Approximately $100 - $150 USD per night
- **Uprising Beach Resort**:
- Location: Pacific Harbour, Viti Levu
- Starting Price: Approximately $150 - $200 USD per night
- **Bamboo Backpackers**:
- Location: Nadi, Viti Levu
- Starting Price: Approximately $50 - $80 USD per night

Cheapest Guesthouses in Fiji:

- **Bamboo Backpackers**:
- Location: Nadi, Viti Levu
- Starting Price: Approximately $20 - $40 USD per night
- **Nadi Downtown Hotel**:
- Location: Nadi, Viti Levu
- Starting Price: Approximately $30 - $50 USD per night
- **Horizon Beach Backpackers Resort**:
- Location: Nadi, Viti Levu
- Starting Price: Approximately $20 - $40 USD per night

Unique and cheap places to stay in Fiji

If you're looking for unique and cheap places to stay in Fiji, consider options such as camping or farm stays. These accommodations offer travelers an opportunity to experience the natural beauty and authentic culture of Fiji while staying within budget. Here are some unique and affordable options:

- **Camping at Natadola Beach**: Natadola Beach, located on the Coral Coast of Viti Levu, offers a picturesque setting for camping under the stars. Many locals and travelers set up tents along the beach for a budget-friendly overnight stay. You can enjoy swimming, snorkeling, and beachcombing during the day and stargazing at night.
- **Farm Stays in the Highlands**: Some farms in the highlands of Viti Levu offer budget-friendly accommodations for travelers looking for a unique experience. You can stay in rustic cottages or guesthouses on the farm and participate in farm activities such as harvesting fruits and vegetables, feeding animals, and learning about traditional Fijian farming techniques.

- **Namosi Eco Retreat**:
    - Situated in the scenic Namosi Highlands, Namosi Eco Retreat offers budget-friendly accommodations in traditional Fijian bures (thatched-roof bungalows) amidst lush tropical surroundings. Guests can engage in farm activities such as organic gardening, fruit picking, and exploring the surrounding forests and waterfalls. The retreat also emphasizes sustainability and community engagement, providing a unique cultural and ecological experience.

- **Homestays in Rural Villages**: Experience authentic Fijian hospitality by staying with local families in rural villages. Many villages offer homestay accommodations where you can immerse yourself in the local culture, participate in traditional ceremonies and activities, and enjoy home-cooked meals. Homestays are usually affordable and provide a genuine cultural exchange experience.
- **Beach Bure Accommodations**: Some beachside resorts and guesthouses offer traditional Fijian bures (thatched-roof huts) for budget-conscious travelers. These bures are often located in scenic beachfront settings and provide basic amenities for a comfortable stay. You can enjoy stunning ocean views, beach access, and a laid-back atmosphere without breaking the bank.
- **Volunteer Accommodations**: If you're interested in volunteering or participating in community projects in Fiji, some organizations offer volunteer accommodations at minimal or no cost. You can contribute to meaningful projects while enjoying affordable lodging and meals provided by the host organization.

- **Vinaka Fiji Volunteer Program**:
    - Vinaka Fiji offers volunteer programs focused on marine conservation and community development. Accommodations for volunteers are typically provided in shared dormitory-style rooms at the organization's base in the

Yasawa Islands. Prices vary depending on the duration of the volunteer program and the specific projects involved.

- **Frontier Fiji Marine Conservation and Community Development Program**:
    - Frontier offers volunteer programs focusing on marine conservation and community development in Fiji. Accommodations for volunteers are typically provided in shared dormitory-style rooms at the organization's research base on a remote island. Prices vary depending on the duration of the program and the specific projects involved.

Enjoy the Finest Five-star Hotels for a 10th of the Cost

If you travel during the peak season or during a major event, you can still enjoy the finest hotels in Fiji for a 10th of the normal cost. With a day pass, you can enjoy all the amenities that the hotel has to offer, including the pool, spa, gym, and included lunches at fine restaurants. This can be a great way to relax and unwind for a day without having to spend money on an overnight stay.

Here are some of the best luxury day passes Fiji hotels:

- **Sheraton Fiji Resort & Spa**:
  - Location: Denarau Island, Nadi
  - Day Pass Price: Approximately $100 - $150 USD per person
  - Features: Access to the resort's pools, beach, non-motorized water sports equipment, and restaurants. Some day passes may include meal or beverage credits.
- **Sofitel Fiji Resort & Spa**:
  - Location: Denarau Island, Nadi
  - Day Pass Price: Approximately $100 - $150 USD per person
  - Features: Access to the resort's pools, beach, non-motorized water sports equipment, and restaurants. Some day passes may include meal or beverage credits.
- **InterContinental Fiji Golf Resort & Spa**:
  - Location: Natadola Bay, Viti Levu
  - Day Pass Price: Approximately $100 - $150 USD per person
  - Features: Access to the resort's pools, beach, non-motorized water sports equipment, and restaurants. Some day passes may include meal or beverage credits.
- **Hilton Fiji Beach Resort & Spa**:
  - Location: Denarau Island, Nadi
  - Day Pass Price: Approximately $100 - $150 USD per person
  - Features: Access to the resort's pools, beach, non-motorized water sports equipment, and restaurants. Some day passes may include meal or beverage credits.
- **The Westin Denarau Island Resort & Spa**:
  - Location: Denarau Island, Nadi
  - Day Pass Price: Approximately $100 - $150 USD per person
  - Features: Access to the resort's pools, beach, non-motorized water sports equipment, and restaurants. Some day passes may include meal or beverage credits.

It's important to note that availability and pricing for day passes may vary depending on the hotel and time of year, so it's always a good idea to check directly with the hotel for the most up-to-date information and to pre-book before your trip to avoid disappointment.

Strategies to Book Five-Star Hotels for Two-Star Prices in Fiji

Use Time

There are two ways to use time. One is to book in advance. Three months will net you the best deal, especially if your visit coincides with an event. The other is to book on the day of your stay. This is a risky move, but if executed well, you can lay your head in a five-star hotel for a 2-star fee.

Before you travel to Fiji, check for big events using a simple google search 'What's on in Fiji', if you find no big events drawing travellers, risk showing up with no accommodation booked (If there are big events on demand exceeds supply and you should avoid using this strategy). If you don't want to risk showing up with no accommodation booked, book a cheap accommodation with free-cancellation.

Before I go into demand-based pricing, take a moment to think about your risk tolerance. By risk, I am not talking about personal safety. No amount of financial savings is worth risking that. What I am talking about is being inconvenienced. Do you deal well with last-minute changes? Can you roll with the punches or do you freak out if something changes? Everyone is different and knowing yourself is the best way to plan a great trip. If you are someone that likes to have everything pre-planned using demand-based pricing to get cheap accommodation will not work for you.

Demand-based pricing

Be they an Airbnb host or hotel manager; no one wants empty rooms. Most will do anything to make some revenue because they still have the same costs to cover whether the room is occupied or not. That's why you will find many hotels drastically slashing room rates for same-day bookings.

How to book five-star hotels for a two-star price

You will not be able to find these discounts when the demand exceeds the supply. So if you're visiting during the peak season, or during an event which has drawn many travellers again don't try this.

1. On the day of your stay, visit booking.com (which offers better discounts than Kayak and agoda.com). Hotel
   Tonight individually checks for any last-minute bookings, but they take a big chunk of the action, so the better deals come from booking.com.
2. The best results come from booking between 2 pm and 4 pm when the risk of losing any revenue with no occupancy is most pronounced, so algorithms supporting hotels slash prices. This is when you can find rates that are not within the "lowest publicly visible" rate.
3. To avoid losing customers to other websites, or cheapening the image of their hotel most will only offer the super cheap rates during a two hour window from 2 pm to 4

pm. Two guests will pay 10x difference in price but it's absolutely vital to the hotel that neither knows it.

Takeaway: To get the lowest price book on the day of stay between 2 pm and 4 pm and extend your search radius to include further afield hotels with good transport connections.

How to trick travel Algorithms to get the lowest hotel price

Do not believe anyone who says changing your IP address to get cheaper hotels or flights does NOT work. If you don't believe us, download a Tor Network and search for flights and hotels to one destination using your current IP and then the tor network (a tor browser hides your IP address from algorithms. It is commonly used by hackers). You will receive different prices.

The price you see is a decision made by an algorithm that adjusts prices using data points such as past bookings, remaining capacity, average demand and the probability of selling the room or flight later at a higher price. If knows you've searched for the area before ip the prices high. To circumvent this, you can either use a different IP address from a cafe or airport or data from an international sim. I use a sim from Three, which provides free data in many countries around the world. When you search from a new IP address, most of the time, and particularly near booking you will get a lower price. Sometimes if your sim comes from a 'rich' country, say the UK or USA, you will see higher rates as the algorithm has learnt people from these countries pay more. The solution is to book from a local wifi connection - but a different one from the one you originally searched from.

- **Use Incognito Mode**: Some travel websites may track your browsing history and show higher prices if they detect repeated searches for the same destination or dates. Using incognito mode or private browsing can help prevent this and may sometimes lead to lower prices.
- **Sign Up for Price Alerts**: Many booking websites offer price alert notifications that notify you when the price of a particular hotel drops. Sign up for these alerts to stay informed about price changes for your desired accommodations.
- **Negotiate Directly with the Hotel**: In some cases, contacting the hotel directly and negotiating the price or asking about special promotions or discounts may result in lower rates, especially for longer stays or during quieter periods.

Cheapest islands to rent an Airbnb

Renting an Airbnb on an island in Fiji can offer a unique and affordable accommodation option for travelers. While prices can vary depending on the location, amenities, and time of year, here are some of the cheapest islands in Fiji where you can find Airbnb rentals with average nightly costs:

- **Viti Levu**:
  - Viti Levu is the largest island in Fiji and offers a range of Airbnb options at varying price points. In less touristy areas or rural villages, you may find more budget-friendly accommodations with average nightly costs ranging from $30 to $100 USD.
- **Vanua Levu**:
  - Vanua Levu is the second-largest island in Fiji and is known for its lush landscapes and authentic Fijian culture. Airbnb rentals on Vanua Levu can be more affordable compared to popular tourist destinations, with average nightly costs ranging from $50 to $150 USD.
- **Taveuni**:
  - Taveuni is often referred to as the "Garden Island" of Fiji due to its rich biodiversity and stunning natural beauty. While Taveuni is a bit more remote, Airbnb rentals on the island can offer excellent value for money, with average nightly costs ranging from $60 to $200 USD.
- **Yasawa Islands**:
  - The Yasawa Islands are a group of remote and pristine islands known for their beautiful beaches and crystal-clear waters. While accommodation options may be limited, Airbnb rentals on some of the Yasawa Islands can be relatively affordable, with average nightly costs ranging from $80 to $250 USD.
- **Mamanuca Islands**:
  - The Mamanuca Islands are a popular tourist destination known for their stunning resorts and picturesque beaches. While accommodation prices in resorts can be high, Airbnb rentals on some of the less-developed islands in the Mamanucas can offer more budget-friendly options, with average nightly costs ranging from $100 to $300 USD.
- **Beqa Island**:
  - Beqa Island is located off the southern coast of Viti Levu and offers a quieter and more laid-back atmosphere compared to some of the more touristy islands. Airbnb rentals on Beqa Island can be affordable, with average nightly costs ranging from $80 to $200 USD.
- **Kadavu Island**:
  - Kadavu Island is known for its pristine reefs, dense rainforests, and traditional Fijian villages. While accommodation options may be limited, Airbnb rentals on Kadavu Island can provide an authentic and budget-friendly experience, with average nightly costs ranging from $70 to $150 USD.

How to get last-minute discounts on owner rented properties

In addition to Airbnb, you can also find owner rented rooms and apartments on www.vrbo.com or HomeAway or a host of others.

Nearly all owners renting accommodation will happily give renters a "last-minute" discount to avoid the space sitting empty, not earning a dime.

Go to Airbnb or another platform and put in today's date. Once you've found something you like start the negotiating by asking for a 25% reduction. A sample message to an Airbnb host might read:

Dear HOST NAME,

I love your apartment. It looks perfect for me. Unfortunately, I'm on a very tight budget. I hope you won't be offended, but I wanted to ask if you would be amenable to offering me a 25% discount for tonight, tomorrow and the following day? I see that you aren't booked. I can assure you, I will leave your place exactly the way I found it. I will put bed linen in the washer and ensure everything is clean for the next guest. I would be delighted to bring you a bottle of wine to thank you for any discount that you could offer.

If this sounds okay, please send me a custom offer, and I will book straight away.

YOUR NAME.

In my experience, a polite, genuine message like this, that proposes reciprocity will be successful 80% of the time. Don't ask for more than 25% off, this person still has to pay the bills and will probably say no as your stay will cost them more in bills than they make. Plus starting higher, can offend the owner and do you want to stay somewhere, where you have offended the host?

In Practice

To use either of these methods, you must travel light. Less stuff means greater mobility, everything is faster and you don't have to check-in or store luggage. If you have a lot of luggage, you're going to have fewer of these opportunities to save on accommodation. Plus travelling light benefits the planet - you're buying, consuming, and transporting less stuff.

Blind-booking

If your risk tolerance does not allow for last-minute booking, you can use blind-booking. Many hotels not wanting to cheapen their brand with known low-prices, choose to operate a blind booking policy. This is where you book without knowing the name of the hotel you're going to stay in until you've made the payment. This is also sometimes used as a marketing strategy where the hotel is seeking to recover from past issues. I've stayed in plenty of blind book hotels. As long as you choose 4 or 5 star hotels, you will find them to be clean, comfortable and safe.

Saving Money on Food in Fiji

Fijian cuisine offers a tantalizing fusion of flavors that reflects the country's rich culinary history. Street food vendors in Fiji typically offer their dishes at much lower prices than restaurants or resorts. For example, a meal of roti with curry from a street vendor might cost around $3 USD, whereas a similar meal at a restaurant could cost upwards of $10 USD. By opting for street food, you can enjoy delicious and filling meals at a fraction of the cost. Exploring Fiji's street food scene is an adventure in itself, offering a delightful array of flavors and culinary treasures that reflect the vibrant culture and diverse heritage of the islands. From savory snacks to sweet treats, here's an in-depth guide to Fiji's street food, complete with starting prices in USD to help you navigate the delicious offerings.

- **Lovo**: Let's start with one of Fiji's most iconic dishes—lovo. Often prepared for special occasions and gatherings, lovo consists of meats, seafood, and vegetables cooked in an underground oven for hours, resulting in tender, smoky flavors. While lovo isn't typically sold as street food, you may come across vendors offering freshly cooked lovo parcels wrapped in banana leaves at local markets or events. Prices can range from $5 to $10 USD per parcel, depending on the size and contents.
- **Roti**: A popular snack found across Fiji, roti is a type of unleavened flatbread that can be enjoyed on its own or paired with savory fillings and condiments. Look for street vendors or small eateries selling freshly cooked roti served with curry, dhal, or chutney. Prices for roti can vary depending on the size and fillings, but you can expect to pay around $1 to $3 USD per piece.
- **Samosa**: Crispy, golden, and bursting with flavor, samosas are a beloved street food snack in Fiji. These triangular pastries are typically filled with spiced potatoes, peas, and sometimes meat, then deep-fried until golden brown. You can find samosa vendors in bustling markets, outside of schools, or at roadside stalls. Prices range from $0.50 to $1.50 USD per samosa, making them an affordable and satisfying snack.
- **Fish and Chips**: With its abundant seafood, Fiji offers some of the freshest and most delicious fish and chips you'll ever taste. Look for food trucks or seaside stalls serving up crispy battered fish alongside hot chips (French fries). Prices for a serving of fish and chips can vary depending on the size of the portion and the type of fish used, but you can expect to pay around $5 to $10 USD per serving.
- **Fijian Curry**: Fijian curry is a flavorful and aromatic dish that reflects the diverse culinary influences of the islands. Made with a blend of spices, coconut milk, and locally sourced ingredients, Fijian curry is often served with rice, roti, or cassava. Look for street food vendors or small eateries offering chicken, fish, or vegetable curry dishes. Prices for a serving of Fijian curry typically range from $5 to $10 USD, depending on the protein and portion size.
- **Kava**: While not technically a food, kava is an integral part of Fijian culture and social gatherings. Made from the root of the kava plant, this traditional drink is known for its relaxing and mildly sedative effects. You can find kava bars or stalls in local markets and villages, where you can join in on a kava session with locals. Prices for a cup of kava can vary depending on the location and quality, but you can expect to pay around $1 to $3 USD per cup.
- **Coconut Treats**: Fiji's abundance of coconuts means you'll find plenty of delicious coconut-based treats sold by street vendors and beachside stalls. From coconut water served in freshly cracked coconuts to coconut desserts like coconut candy and coconut ice cream, there's something to satisfy every coconut lover's craving.

Prices for coconut treats vary depending on the type and size of the serving, but you can expect to pay around $1 to $5 USD per item.

- **Pani Popo**: Originating from Fiji's Pacific Island neighbors, pani popo is a sweet and indulgent treat that has found its way into Fiji's street food scene. This dessert consists of soft, sweet bread rolls soaked in a rich coconut cream sauce, creating a decadent and comforting delicacy. Look for street vendors or bakeries selling freshly baked pani popo, typically priced at around $1 to $3 USD per roll.

Cheapest Champagne Bars:

- **Cloud 9 Fiji**:
    - Location: Malolo Barrier Reef, Mamanuca Islands
    - Cloud 9 Fiji is a floating bar and pizzeria located in the middle of the ocean. While they don't offer traditional champagne, they serve a selection of sparkling wines and cocktails in a stunning setting. Prices for drinks vary, but they typically offer affordable options for enjoying a drink in a unique environment.
- **Port Denarau Marina**:
    - Location: Denarau Island, Nadi
    - Port Denarau Marina is home to several bars and restaurants offering a range of beverage options, including champagne and sparkling wines. While prices may vary depending on the establishment, you can often find affordable drink specials and happy hour deals.

Cheap Tasting Menus:

- **The Rhum-Ba at Musket Cove Island Resort & Marina**:
- Location: Malolo Lailai Island, Mamanuca Islands
- The Rhum-Ba offers a diverse menu of Fijian and international cuisine, including seafood, grilled meats, and vegetarian options. While they may not offer traditional tasting menus, you can create your own tasting experience by ordering a variety of small plates to share with friends or family.

Unusual Restaurants with Great Prices:

- **Nakelo Treasure Island Floating Restaurant**:
    - Location: Nadi Bay, Viti Levu
    - Nakelo Treasure Island is a floating restaurant located in Nadi Bay, offering stunning views of the surrounding waters. They serve a variety of Fijian and international dishes at affordable prices, including seafood, curries, and grilled meats.
- **Bamboo Restaurant & Bar**:
    - Location: Navini Island, Mamanuca Islands
    - Bamboo Restaurant & Bar is located on Navini Island and offers a unique dining experience on the beach. They serve fresh seafood, grilled meats, and vegetarian dishes at reasonable prices, allowing guests to enjoy a memorable meal in a picturesque setting.

Cheapest Supermarkets:

- **RB Patel Supermarket**:
    - RB Patel is a popular supermarket chain in Fiji with multiple locations across the islands. They offer a wide range of groceries, fresh produce, and household items at competitive prices. Look for specials and promotions to get even better deals on groceries.
- **NewWorld Supermarket**:

- NewWorld is another well-known supermarket chain in Fiji, offering affordable groceries and everyday essentials. They have various locations in major cities and towns, providing convenience and value for shoppers.

Breakfast Under $5:

- **Bread and Fruit from Local Markets**: Visit a local market such as Suva Municipal Market or Nadi Produce Market and pick up a loaf of freshly baked bread or a selection of tropical fruits like bananas, papayas, and pineapples for a quick and nutritious breakfast. Prices for these items are typically very affordable, allowing you to enjoy a filling breakfast for under $5.
- **Roti with Curry**: Head to a nearby Indian eatery or food stall and order a simple roti with curry. Roti is a popular Indian flatbread that pairs perfectly with spicy curry sauce. You can usually find roti with vegetarian or meat-based curry fillings for under $5, making it a satisfying and budget-friendly breakfast option.

Lunch Under $5:

- **Noodle Soup from a Food Stall**: Look for food stalls or small eateries serving noodle soup, such as Fijian-style lovo or Chinese-style noodle soups. These hearty and flavorful soups are often available for under $5 and come with a variety of toppings such as vegetables, chicken, pork, or seafood, providing a filling and affordable lunch option.
- **Samosa with Chutney**: Visit an Indian snack stall or bakery and order a couple of samosas with chutney. Samosas are deep-fried pastries filled with spiced potatoes, peas, and sometimes meat. They're a popular snack in Fiji and are usually available for under $5 for a couple, making them an affordable and tasty lunchtime treat.

Dinner Under $5:

- **Rourou (Taro Leaf) Curry**: Look for local Fijian eateries or food stalls serving traditional dishes like rourou curry. Rourou is a type of taro leaf commonly used in Fijian cooking, and it's often prepared in a creamy coconut milk curry sauce. You can typically find a serving of rourou curry with rice for under $5, providing a satisfying and budget-friendly dinner option.
- **Fried Rice or Noodles**: Visit a Chinese food stall or eatery and order a serving of fried rice or noodles. These dishes are often available with a choice of vegetables, chicken, pork, or seafood and are served in generous portions for under $5, making them an excellent value option for dinner.

Best value all you can eat restaurants

- **Grand Pacific Hotel** (Suva, Viti Levu):
  - The Grand Pacific Hotel in Suva occasionally hosts themed all-you-can-eat buffets at its renowned restaurant, offering a wide selection of Fijian and international dishes. Keep an eye out for special promotions and events for an opportunity to enjoy a lavish buffet spread with excellent value for money.
- **The Warwick Fiji** (Coral Coast, Viti Levu):

- The Warwick Fiji, a luxury resort on the Coral Coast, hosts regular buffet dinners at its various restaurants, including the Bula Brasserie and Wicked Walu Seafood Restaurant. These buffets feature a diverse array of cuisines, including Fijian, Asian, and Western dishes, providing excellent value for guests looking to indulge in all-you-can-eat dining.
- **Radisson Blu Resort Fiji Denarau Island** (Denarau Island, Viti Levu):
  - The Radisson Blu Resort on Denarau Island offers all-day dining options at its various restaurants, including Blu Bar & Grill and Chantara Thai Restaurant. While they may not have traditional all-you-can-eat buffets, they often have themed buffet nights with unlimited servings of selected dishes, providing guests with excellent value for money.
- **Sheraton Fiji Resort** (Denarau Island, Viti Levu):
  - The Sheraton Fiji Resort on Denarau Island hosts regular buffet dinners at its Feast Restaurant, featuring a wide selection of Fijian, Asian, and international cuisines. Guests can enjoy unlimited servings of dishes such as seafood, meats, salads, and desserts, making it a great value dining option for families and groups.
- **InterContinental Fiji Golf Resort & Spa** (Natadola Bay, Viti Levu):
  - The InterContinental Fiji Resort & Spa offers buffet-style dining at its various restaurants, including Sanasana Restaurant and Navo Restaurant. While they may not have all-you-can-eat buffets every day, they often host special buffet nights with themed cuisines and unlimited servings, providing guests with excellent value for money.

Best Desserts in Fiji:

- **Coconut Tart (Tavola)**:
  - Coconut tarts, locally known as "tavola," are a popular dessert in Fiji. These sweet treats consist of a crispy pastry shell filled with a creamy coconut filling made from freshly grated coconut, sugar, and sometimes spices like cardamom or vanilla. Coconut tarts are a beloved Fijian dessert enjoyed during celebrations and special occasions, showcasing the island's abundant coconut harvest and rich culinary heritage.
- **Pineapple Pie**:
  - Pineapple pie is another favorite dessert in Fiji, featuring a buttery pie crust filled with sweet and tangy pineapple filling. This tropical twist on a classic pie is a refreshing treat on a hot day and highlights Fiji's abundance of fresh fruits, including pineapples grown locally on the islands.

Best Bakeries in Fiji:

- **Hot Bread Kitchen**:
  - Hot Bread Kitchen is a popular bakery chain in Fiji with locations across the islands. They offer a wide range of freshly baked goods, including bread, pastries, cakes, and savory snacks, made using high-quality ingredients and traditional recipes. Their warm and fluffy roti rolls are a local favorite and perfect for a quick breakfast or snack on the go.
- **Bulaccino Café & Bakery**:

- Bulaccino Café & Bakery is a charming bakery and café located in Nadi, Fiji. They specialize in artisanal bread, pastries, and desserts, made from scratch using locally sourced ingredients. Their selection of sweet treats, including cakes, tarts, and cookies, are perfect for indulging your sweet tooth while enjoying a cup of freshly brewed coffee.

Prettiest Cafes in Fiji:

- **Gourmet Fiji**:
  - Gourmet Fiji is a picturesque café located in Denarau Island, Fiji. Set in a lush garden setting with outdoor seating, this café offers a tranquil atmosphere perfect for enjoying breakfast, brunch, or afternoon tea. Their menu features a variety of gourmet dishes, including freshly baked pastries, sandwiches, salads, and specialty coffee drinks.
- **Café O Fiji**:
  - Café O Fiji is a stylish café situated in Suva, Fiji's capital city. With its chic décor, comfortable seating, and vibrant ambiance, this café is a popular spot for locals and tourists alike. They serve a variety of light meals, coffee, and desserts, making it an ideal place to relax and unwind after a day of exploring the city.

Happy Hours in Fiji:

Happy Hours can save you a small fortune in Fiji. Here are some popular spots known for their happy hour specials on each major Fiji island:

- **Viti Levu**:
  - **Port Denarau Marina, Nadi**: Several bars and restaurants along the marina offer happy hour specials with scenic views of the waterfront.
  - **Coral Coast**: Resorts and beachfront bars along the Coral Coast, such as The Warwick Fiji and Outrigger Fiji Beach Resort, often have happy hour promotions with discounted drinks.
  - **Suva**: The capital city of Suva boasts a lively nightlife scene with various bars and pubs offering happy hour deals. Check out venues like Bad Dog Cafe or Traps Bar for specials.
- **Vanua Levu**:
  - **Savusavu**: The picturesque town of Savusavu features waterfront bars and restaurants where you can enjoy happy hour drinks while watching the sunset over the bay.
  - **Labasa**: Look for local pubs and bars in Labasa that may offer happy hour specials, catering to both residents and visitors.
- **Yasawa Islands**:
  - **Barefoot Manta Island Resort**: This eco-friendly resort on Drawaqa Island occasionally offers happy hour specials at its beachside bar, providing a relaxed atmosphere to enjoy drinks after a day of snorkeling or diving.
  - **Navutu Stars Resort**: Located on Yaqeta Island, Navutu Stars Resort may have happy hour promotions at its beachfront bar, allowing guests to sip cocktails while admiring the stunning ocean views.
- **Mamanuca Islands**:

- **Malolo Island Resort**: This family-friendly resort may offer happy hour specials at its beachfront bar, perfect for enjoying cocktails with your toes in the sand.
- **Musket Cove Island Resort**: Look out for happy hour deals at Musket Cove's Trader Café or Island Bar, where you can unwind with drinks overlooking the marina or lagoon.

Unique Beers in Fiji:

- **Fiji Gold**:
    - Fiji Gold is a popular local beer brewed by Fiji Brewery Limited. It's a light and refreshing lager with a smooth taste, making it a favorite among locals and visitors alike. While Fiji Gold is widely available throughout the islands, its unique flavor and connection to Fiji's brewing traditions make it a must-try for beer enthusiasts.
- **Vonu Beer**:
    - Vonu Beer is another local favorite brewed in Fiji. Named after the Fijian word for turtle, Vonu Beer is crafted using pure Fijian water and high-quality ingredients, resulting in a crisp and flavorful lager. Look for Vonu Beer at bars, restaurants, and supermarkets across the islands for a taste of Fiji's craft brewing scene.

Cheapest Beer Tastings in Fiji:

- **Brewery Tours**:
    - Fiji Brewery Limited or Paradise Beverages for information on tours and tastings, as they may offer affordable packages for visitors interested in exploring Fiji's beer culture from $10.

Itinerary for first time visitor to Fiji

Day 1: Arrival in Nadi

- Arrive at Nadi International Airport.
- Take a local bus or shared taxi to your accommodation in Nadi or nearby Denarau Island.
- Check-in at a budget hostel or guesthouse. Budget: $20 - $30 USD per night.
- Spend the day exploring Nadi town, visiting the local markets, and enjoying inexpensive street food. Budget: $10 - $15 USD for meals.

Day 2: Explore Nadi

- Visit the Garden of the Sleeping Giant. Entrance fee: $10 - $15 USD.
- Relax at a nearby beach or public park.
- Enjoy dinner at a local eatery or cook your own meal at the hostel. Budget: $10 - $15 USD for meals.

Day 3: Beach Day at Wailoaloa Beach

- Take a local bus or taxi to Wailoaloa Beach, a popular spot near Nadi.
- Spend the day swimming, sunbathing, and relaxing on the beach. Bring your own snacks and drinks to save money. Budget: $5 - $10 USD for transportation.
- Enjoy a sunset walk along the beach.
- Return to your accommodation for a budget-friendly dinner. Budget: $10 - $15 USD for meals.

Day 4: Day Trip to the Sabeto Mud Pools

- Join a budget-friendly group tour or take a local bus to the Sabeto Mud Pools and Hot Springs. Tour prices vary, but budget around $20 - $30 USD per person.
- Enjoy a therapeutic mud bath and soak in the natural hot springs.
- Return to Nadi in the afternoon and explore more of the town.
- Have dinner at a local restaurant or street food stall. Budget: $10 - $15 USD for meals.

Day 5: Travel to Suva

- Take a local bus or shared taxi to Suva, the capital city of Fiji. Budget: $15 - $20 USD for transportation.
- Check into a budget hostel or guesthouse in Suva. Budget: $20 - $30 USD per night.
- Explore Suva's downtown area, including the municipal market and historic landmarks.
- Have dinner at a cheap eatery or try some local street food. Budget: $10 - $15 USD for meals.

Day 6: Cultural Exploration in Suva

- Visit the Fiji Museum and Thurston Gardens. Entrance fees: $5 - $10 USD.
- Explore the Colo-i-Suva Forest Park and go for a nature walk. Entrance fee: $5 - $10 USD.
- Have lunch at a budget-friendly restaurant in Suva. Budget: $10 - $15 USD for meals.
- Spend the afternoon relaxing at your accommodation or exploring more of Suva.
- Enjoy a budget-friendly dinner at a local eatery. Budget: $10 - $15 USD for meals.

Day 7: Departure from Fiji

- Check out of your accommodation and head to Suva's bus station or airport.
- Take a bus or shared taxi back to Nadi International Airport. Budget: $15 - $20 USD for transportation.
- Depart Fiji with fond memories of your budget-friendly adventure.

Total Estimated Budget for 7 Days: $360

Itinerary for 14 days

Day 1-3: Nadi and Denarau Island

Day 1: Arrival in Nadi

- Arrive at Nadi International Airport and transfer to your accommodation.
- Check-in at a budget-friendly luxury resort or boutique hotel in Nadi or Denarau Island. Consider options like Bamboo Backpackers on Denarau Island with prices starting at $30 USD per night.
- Enjoy a leisurely stroll along Denarau Beach, taking in the sunset and ocean views.

Day 2: Explore Nadi

- Visit the Garden of the Sleeping Giant to admire exotic orchids and tropical flora. Entrance fee is $15 USD.
- Explore the local markets in Nadi town, shopping for souvenirs and handicrafts.
- Indulge in a traditional Fijian feast at a local restaurant, sampling dishes like kokoda and lovo. Budget around $20 - $30 USD for a meal.

Day 3: Day Trip to Mamanuca Islands

- Take a day trip to the Mamanuca Islands, known for their pristine beaches and crystal-clear waters. Consider the South Sea Cruises day trip which costs around $100 USD per person.
- Relax on the beach, snorkel among colorful coral reefs, or enjoy water sports like kayaking and paddleboarding.
- Return to Nadi in the evening and unwind with a cocktail by the pool at your resort.

Day 4-7: Coral Coast and Pacific Harbour

Day 4: Transfer to Coral Coast

- Depart for the Coral Coast, known for its stunning beaches and lush rainforests.
- Check into a luxury eco-resort or beachfront villa overlooking the Pacific Ocean. Consider the Coral Coast Resort with prices starting at $50 USD per night.
- Spend the afternoon relaxing by the pool or exploring the resort's amenities.

Day 5: Adventure in Pacific Harbour

- Participate in adrenaline-pumping activities like zip-lining, white-water rafting, or shark diving. Budget around $50 - $100 USD depending on the activity.
- Visit the Arts Village and Cultural Centre to learn about Fijian traditions and crafts. Entrance fee is $10 USD.
- Enjoy a traditional Fijian lovo lunch, featuring roasted meats and seafood cooked in an underground oven. Budget around $20 - $30 USD for lunch.

Day 6: Wellness Retreat

- Indulge in a rejuvenating spa experience, choosing from a range of massages and treatments. Budget around $50 - $100 USD for a spa treatment.
- Practice yoga or meditation by the beach, immersing yourself in the tranquility of Fiji's natural surroundings.
- Dine at the resort's fine dining restaurant, savoring a multi-course tasting menu inspired by local ingredients. Budget around $30 - $50 USD for dinner.

Day 7: Explore Suva

- Depart for Suva, the capital city of Fiji, located on the southeastern coast of Viti Levu. Consider taking a local bus for budget-friendly transportation.
- Visit the Fiji Museum, Thurston Gardens, and Colo-i-Suva Forest Park. Entrance fees range from $5 - $10 USD.
- Check into a luxury boutique hotel or heritage guesthouse in Suva. Consider options like Southern Cross Hotel with prices starting at $40 USD per night.

Day 8-11: Taveuni Island and Garden Island Resort

Day 8: Flight to Taveuni Island

- Take a domestic flight from Nadi to Taveuni Island, known as the "Garden Island" for its lush rainforests and waterfalls. Budget around $200 - $300 USD for a one-way flight.
- Check into the Garden Island Resort, a luxury boutique resort overlooking the Somosomo Strait. Prices start at $100 USD per night.

Day 9: Waterfall Hike

- Embark on a guided hike to Tavoro Waterfalls in Bouma National Heritage Park. Consider joining a guided tour for around $20 USD.
- Swim in natural pools beneath the waterfalls and picnic in the pristine rainforest surroundings.
- Return to the resort in the afternoon and relax with a spa treatment or massage. Budget around $50 - $100 USD for a spa treatment.

Day 10: Snorkeling and Diving

- Explore the vibrant coral reefs and marine life surrounding Taveuni Island.
- Snorkel or scuba dive at Rainbow Reef, known for its kaleidoscope of colors and diverse marine ecosystem. Prices for snorkeling or diving tours vary but budget around $50 - $100 USD.
- Enjoy a beachfront barbecue dinner at the resort, feasting on fresh seafood and local specialties. Budget around $20 - $30 USD for dinner.

Day 11: Cultural Experience

- Visit local villages on Taveuni Island to learn about Fijian culture and traditions. Consider arranging a village tour for around $20 - $30 USD.
- Participate in traditional ceremonies, crafts, and activities with local villagers.
- Attend a Fijian meke performance in the evening, featuring music, dance, and storytelling. Look out for cultural shows at the resort or nearby villages.

Day 12-14: Return to Nadi and Departure

Day 12: Flight to Nadi

- Take a domestic flight back to Nadi and transfer to your accommodation. Budget around $100 USD for a one-way flight.
- Spend the afternoon shopping for souvenirs and last-minute gifts in Nadi town.
- Enjoy a farewell dinner at a waterfront restaurant, toasting to your unforgettable journey in Fiji. Budget around $20 - $30 USD for dinner.

Day 13: Relaxation and Leisure

- Spend your final full day in Fiji relaxing by the pool or on the beach, soaking up the sun and serenity.
- Indulge in one last spa treatment or massage to unwind before your departure. Budget around $50 - $100 USD for a spa treatment.

Unique bargains we love in Fiji

The local markets offer an abundance of juicy tropical fruits and vegetables at bargain prices. And the best part? You'll be supporting local farmers and artisans with every purchase, making it a win-win for both your taste buds and the community.

But Fiji's bargains go beyond just fresh produce. For those with a thirst for adventure, the island offers a plethora of unique experiences that won't break the bank. How about embarking on a village tour or homestay to immerse yourself in Fijian culture? For around $20 to $30 per person, you can participate in guided tours that include cultural demonstrations, visits to local homes, and traditional ceremonies. Homestay experiences, on the other hand, typically range from $40 to $60 per night, offering accommodation, meals, and interactions with locals—all at bargain prices that make for unforgettable memories.

And let's not forget about the culinary delights that await in Fiji. While luxury dining experiences can be pricey, there are plenty of hidden gems where you can savor authentic Fijian flavors without breaking the bank. From roadside food stalls serving up mouthwatering curries to local eateries dishing out freshly caught seafood, the options are endless. And of course, no trip to Fiji would be complete without indulging in locally brewed beer and Fijian rum, available at reasonable prices that make every sip a bargain worth toasting to.

Snapshot: How to have a $5,000 trip to Fiji on a $500

Expense Category	**Estimated Cost (USD)**
Airfare	$300
Accommodation	$20-$50 per night
Ferries	$50-$100
Food and Dining	$10-$20 per day
Activities and Excursions	$50-$100
Miscellaneous Expenses	$20-$50
Total Estimated Cost	**$350-$570**

OUR SUPER CHEAP TIPS...

Here are our specific super cheap tips for enjoying a $5,000 trip to Fiji for just $500.

Arriving

There are two main international airports in Fiji:

- **Nadi International Airport (NAN)**:
  - Location: Nadi, on the western side of Viti Levu.
  - How to Get to the City Cheaply: From Nadi International Airport, the most budget-friendly way to get to the city is by taking a public bus. The local bus terminal is located just outside the airport, and you can catch buses to various destinations across the island. Bus fares typically start at around FJD $1-2. Alternatively, you can opt for shared airport shuttles or private taxis for a slightly higher cost, with prices starting from FJD $10-20 depending on your destination.

- **Nausori International Airport (SUV)**:
  - Location: Nausori, near Suva on the eastern side of Viti Levu.
  - How to Get to the City Cheaply: From Nausori International Airport, you can also take public buses to Suva and other nearby towns. The bus stop is located just outside the airport terminal, and fares are relatively inexpensive, starting from around FJD $1-2. Shared airport shuttles and private taxis are also available for those looking for more convenience, with prices starting from FJD $10-20 depending on your destination.

Getting Around

Buses

Buses are the most common and affordable mode of public transportation in Fiji. They operate on major islands like Viti Levu and Vanua Levu, connecting towns, villages, and tourist destinations. Here's a breakdown of bus transportation in Fiji:

- **Types of Buses:** There are two types of buses in Fiji: local buses (known as "buses") and express buses (known as "expresses"). Local buses make frequent stops, while express buses operate on specific routes with fewer stops, making them faster.
- **Fares:** Bus fares vary depending on the distance traveled, but they're generally affordable, ranging from FJD $1 to $10, depending on the route. Exact change is required when boarding.
- **Bus Terminals:** Major towns like Nadi, Suva, and Lautoka have central bus terminals where you can catch buses to various destinations. These terminals also serve as hubs for intercity and long-distance travel.
- **Travel Tips:** Keep in mind that buses may not always adhere to strict schedules, so be prepared to wait a bit longer during peak hours. Additionally, buses can get crowded, especially during rush hours, so consider traveling during off-peak times for a more comfortable experience.
- Fijians are renowned for their hospitality, and they'll gladly assist you in navigating the routes and destinations.
- Keep an eye out for the occasional stop at roadside stalls, where you can sample delicious Fijian snacks like cassava chips, coconut bread, or freshly cut pineapple. Trust me; your taste buds will thank you for the culinary adventure.

Cheapest Island Hopping

The cheapest way to island hop in Fiji is by utilizing ferry services operated by companies like South Sea Cruises. These ferries offer regular services between the main island of Viti Levu and various islands in the Yasawa and Mamanuca island groups.

While prices may vary depending on the route and the specific ferry operator, here are some examples of local ferry services along with approximate prices in USD:

- **South Sea Cruises**: South Sea Cruises operates ferry services between the main islands of Fiji, including Viti Levu, the Mamanuca Islands, and the Yasawa Islands. Prices for ferry tickets vary depending on the route and the type of service (standard or high-speed). As of the last available information, prices typically start from around $30 to $50 USD for one-way tickets between Viti Levu and the nearby islands.
- **Awesome Adventures Fiji**: Awesome Adventures Fiji offers ferry services to the Yasawa Islands, providing travelers with access to some of Fiji's most beautiful and remote islands. The ferry service operates regular departures from Denarau Marina on Viti Levu to various Yasawa Islands. Prices for ferry tickets start from approximately $60 to $100 USD for one-way trips, depending on the destination and the type of ticket (standard or premium).
- **Goundar Shipping**: Goundar Shipping is a local ferry operator that provides transportation services between the main islands of Fiji, including Viti Levu and Vanua Levu. The company offers affordable ferry options for both passengers and vehicles. Prices for ferry tickets on Goundar Shipping vary depending on the route, the type of ticket (economy or cabin class), and whether you are traveling as a passenger or with a vehicle. Prices for passenger tickets typically start from around $20 to $40 USD for one-way trips between Viti Levu and Vanua Levu.
- **Sunbeam Transport**: Sunbeam Transport operates ferry services between Viti Levu and various islands in the Lau Group, providing transportation for passengers and cargo. While prices may vary depending on the specific destination and the type of ticket, fares for ferry services with Sunbeam Transport generally start from around $50 to $100 USD for one-way trips.

Car Rentals

Renting a car is a convenient option for exploring Fiji at your own pace, allowing you to access remote areas and off-the-beaten-path destinations. Here's what you need to know about car rentals in Fiji:

- **Cost:** Car rental prices vary depending on the vehicle type, rental duration, and insurance coverage. Daily rates start at around FJD $50 for a basic compact car and can go up to FJD $150 or more for larger vehicles.
- **Driving Tips:** Fiji drives on the left side of the road, and road conditions can vary, especially in rural areas. It's essential to drive cautiously and be mindful of local traffic laws and regulations.

Bike Rentals

Renting a bike is an excellent way to explore Fiji's towns, villages, and scenic landscapes. Here's what you need to know about bike rentals:

- **Rental Shops:** Bike rental shops are available in major tourist areas and towns across Fiji, offering a variety of bicycles for rent, including mountain bikes, cruisers, and e-bikes.
- **Cost:** Bike rental prices vary depending on the type of bike and rental duration. Daily rates start at around FJD $10 for basic bikes and can go up to FJD $50 or more for premium models.

Sample Chart of Transportation Options and Starting Prices:

Mode of Transportation	Description	Starting Price (FJD)
Local Bus	Regular buses with multiple stops	$1
Express Bus	Faster buses with limited stops	$2
Passenger Ferry	Ferry for passengers between islands	$20
Cargo Ferry	Ferry for transporting goods and vehicles	$10
Car Rental	Rental of a compact car for one day	$50
Bike Rental	Rental of a basic bike for one day	$10

Top paid attractions in Fiji on the cheap

Tavoro Waterfalls

These cascading beauties are nestled within the lush landscapes of Bouma National Heritage Park on Taveuni Island.

The starting price for entry is approximately $10 USD. Alternatively, you can explore nearby natural pools and smaller waterfalls for free, offering a similar refreshing experience.

Getting There:

First things first, you'll need to get to Taveuni Island. You can either take a domestic flight from Nadi or Suva to Matei Airport on Taveuni, or you can opt for a ferry ride from Viti Levu. Once you're on Taveuni, you'll need to make your way to Bouma National Heritage Park, where the waterfalls are located. You can hire a taxi, rent a car, or take a local bus for $1.

Once you arrive at Bouma National Heritage Park, get ready to immerse yourself in nature. The park is a tropical paradise, filled with lush rainforests, vibrant flora, and diverse wildlife. Take your time to soak in the beauty of the surroundings as you make your way to the waterfalls, here are the highlights:

Flora:

- **Rainforest Majesty:** Prepare to be mesmerized by the towering canopy of ancient rainforest that blankets much of Bouma National Heritage Park. Here, you'll find an exquisite tapestry of plant life, including towering mahogany trees, majestic banyans, and delicate ferns draping from branches.
- **Botanical Marvels:** Keep your eyes peeled for a dazzling array of tropical flora, from vibrant orchids in all shapes and colors to exotic blooms like heliconias and hibiscus. Marvel at the intricate patterns of giant ferns and the glossy leaves of tropical palms as you wander along the park's winding trails.
- **Rare Gems:** Bouma National Heritage Park is home to several rare and endemic plant species found nowhere else on Earth. Look out for the Tagimoucia flower, a stunning red and white blossom revered as Fiji's national flower and found only on the slopes of Taveuni.

Fauna:

- **Avian Symphony:** With over 100 species of birds calling the park home, birdwatching enthusiasts are in for a treat. Listen to the melodious calls of the orange dove, the vibrant plumage of the Fiji parrotfinch, and the distinctive cry of the silktail echoing through the forest.

- **Reef Residents:** While Bouma National Heritage Park is renowned for its terrestrial beauty, its marine realm is equally captivating. Dive beneath the crystal-clear waters to encounter a kaleidoscope of marine life, from colorful reef fish darting among coral gardens to graceful sea turtles gliding through the depths.

The hike to Tavoro Waterfalls is a memorable experience in itself. The trail winds through the rainforest, crossing streams and traversing rugged terrain. It's a moderate hike, so be sure to wear comfortable shoes and bring plenty of water. Along the way, keep an eye out for native birds and tropical plants – you might even spot a friendly iguana or two!

After about a 20 to 30-minute hike (depending on your pace), you'll arrive at Tavoro Waterfalls. Get ready to be awestruck by the sight of the cascading water against the backdrop of the lush greenery. Take a moment to soak it all in – you've earned it! If you're feeling adventurous, you can even take a refreshing dip in the natural pool at the base of the falls.

Tips for Visiting:

- Visit during weekdays or off-peak seasons to avoid crowds and save on entrance fees.
- Wear sturdy shoes with good grip, as the trails can be muddy and slippery, especially after rainfall.
- Don't forget to bring insect repellent – those jungle critters can be pesky!

Sri Siva Subramaniya Temple

Located in Nadi, this colorful Hindu temple is a cultural gem. There is a small entrance fee, typically around $5 USD. As a free alternative, stroll through the temple's exterior and appreciate its intricate architecture and vibrant decorations. Practical tip: Dress modestly and remove shoes before entering. The temple, built in the traditional Dravidian style, is the largest of its kind in the Southern Hemisphere.

Getting There:

The temple is located in Nadi, so if you're flying into Fiji, chances are you'll land at Nadi International Airport. From there, you can easily reach the temple by bus.

Exploring the Temple:

Once you arrive, prepare to be dazzled by the vibrant colors and intricate architecture of the Sri Siva Subramaniya Temple. It's a cultural gem that offers a glimpse into Fiji's rich Hindu heritage.

Tips for Visiting:

- Dress modestly and remove your shoes before entering the temple grounds.
- Consider joining a group tour or visiting during festivals for a more immersive experience.
- Take some time to stroll around the exterior of the temple and admire its beauty from all angles.

Natadola Beach

With its pristine sands and azure waters, Natadola Beach is a paradise for sun-seekers. Access to the beach is generally free, but there are fees for activities like horseback riding or snorkeling. To save, bring your own beach gear and pack a picnic. Alternatively, explore nearby less-known beaches like Korolevu or Yanuca for a quieter experience. Practical tip: Apply sunscreen liberally and stay hydrated. Natadola Beach holds significance as a filming location for the movie "Cast Away," starring Tom Hanks.

Getting There:

Natadola Beach is located on the main island of Viti Levu, near the town of Sigatoka. You can reach it by taxi, rental car, or even local bus from Nadi or Suva.

Exploring the Beach:

Once you arrive, you'll be greeted by pristine white sands and crystal-clear turquoise waters. Natadola Beach is perfect for swimming, sunbathing, and water sports like snorkeling and horseback riding.

Tips for Visiting:

- Bring your own beach gear and pack a picnic to save money on food and drinks.
- Consider exploring nearby less-known beaches like Korolevu or Yanuca for a quieter experience.

Kula Eco Park

This conservation park near Sigatoka showcases Fiji's native flora and fauna. There's an admission fee, starting at $20 USD approximately. To save, consider purchasing tickets online in advance or looking for discounts through hotel packages. As a free alternative, embark on nature walks in nearby Sigatoka Sand Dunes National Park, where you might spot indigenous wildlife like the Fiji crested iguana.

Visit early in the day to catch the animal feeding sessions. The park plays a vital role in preserving endangered Fijian species.

Kula Eco Park is located near Sigatoka on the main island of Viti Levu in Fiji. You can reach it by taxi, rental car, or local bus from Nadi or Suva.

Once you arrive, you'll step into a world of Fijian biodiversity. Kula Eco Park showcases Fiji's native flora and fauna, including colorful birds, reptiles, and tropical plants.

Tips for Visiting:

- There's an admission fee to enter the park, but you can save by purchasing tickets online in advance or looking for discounts through hotel packages.
- Don't miss the animal feeding sessions, which are a highlight of the park experience.
- If you're looking for a free alternative, consider exploring nearby Sigatoka Sand Dunes National Park for nature walks and wildlife spotting.

Sabeto Hot Springs and Mud Pool

Located near Nadi, these natural geothermal springs offer relaxation and rejuvenation. There's an entrance fee, usually around $15 USD. For a free alternative, you can soak in the therapeutic mud pools at low tide along the coastlines of Sabeto. Practical tip: Bring a change of clothes and a towel. The hot springs have been used for centuries by Fijians for their healing properties.

Garden of the Sleeping Giant

This botanical garden in Nadi boasts a stunning collection of orchids and tropical plants. There's an admission fee, starting at $15 USD approximately. To save, visit during the early morning hours for discounted entry or purchase combined tickets if you plan to visit other nearby attractions. As a free alternative, explore the lush landscapes of Koroyanitu National Heritage Park, where you can hike amidst native flora and fauna. Practical tip: Wear comfortable shoes and carry water. The garden was once the private collection of the late Raymond Burr, an American actor.

Getting There:

The Garden of the Sleeping Giant is located near Nadi on the main island of Viti Levu in Fiji. You can reach it by local bus

Once you arrive, you'll find yourself surrounded by lush landscapes and stunning collections of orchids and tropical plants. It's a tranquil oasis perfect for nature lovers and photography enthusiasts.

Beqa Island

Known for its spectacular diving sites, Beqa Island offers an underwater paradise teeming with marine life. While diving and snorkeling excursions can be pricey, consider booking with local operators for competitive rates or visiting during the off-peak season for discounts. As a free alternative, explore the island's pristine beaches and go beachcombing for unique seashells and driftwood. Practical tip: Bring your own snorkeling gear if possible to save on rental costs. Beqa Island has a rich history of traditional fire-walking ceremonies, believed to originate from ancestral spirits.

Getting There:

Beqa Island is located off the southern coast of Viti Levu, Fiji's main island. The cheapest way to get there is by taking a boat from Pacific Harbour, which is located on the southern coast of Viti Levu. You can join a group tour to Beqa Island.

Once you arrive, you'll be greeted by pristine beaches, vibrant coral reefs, and lush rainforest. Beqa Island is known for its spectacular diving sites, so be sure to bring your snorkeling gear or book a diving excursion to explore the underwater wonders.

Tips for Visiting:

- While accommodations on Beqa Island can be pricey, you can save money by opting for budget-friendly guesthouses or backpacker lodges.
- Consider booking your accommodation and transportation as part of a package deal to save money on overall costs.
- If you're looking for a free alternative, spend your days exploring the island's pristine beaches and going beachcombing for unique seashells and driftwood.

Denarau Island

This man-made island near Nadi is a hub for luxury resorts, shopping, and dining. While accommodations can be pricey, you can save by booking in advance and looking for package deals that include activities or meals. As a free alternative, enjoy the public beaches on Denarau and take leisurely walks along the waterfront promenade. Practical tip: Explore the island's marina area for affordable dining options. Denarau Island was developed in the 1960s and has since become a premier tourist destination in Fiji.

Getting There:

Denarau Island is located near Nadi on the main island of Viti Levu in Fiji. You can reach it by taxi, rental car, or shuttle bus from Nadi International Airport or other areas in Viti Levu.

Once you arrive, you'll find yourself surrounded by luxury resorts, shopping centers, and dining options. Denarau Island is a hub for relaxation and entertainment, offering everything from pristine beaches to championship golf courses.

Tips for Visiting:

- While accommodations on Denarau Island can be pricey, you can save money by booking in advance and looking for package deals that include activities or meals.
- Enjoy the public beaches on Denarau, which are free to access, and take leisurely walks along the waterfront promenade.
- Explore the island's marina area for affordable dining options and scenic views of the ocean.

Fiji Museum

Located in Suva, the Fiji Museum offers insight into the country's rich cultural heritage. While there's an admission fee, you can save by visiting on Thursdays when entry is half-price or by purchasing a combination ticket with other nearby attractions. As a free alternative, explore Suva's historic Albert Park and Thurston Gardens, which offer glimpses into Fiji's colonial past and lush botanical wonders. Practical tip: Engage with museum guides for fascinating insights into Fijian history and culture. The museum's collection includes artifacts dating back over 3,000 years.

The Fiji Museum is located in Suva, the capital city of Fiji, on the main island of Viti Levu. You can reach it by taxi, rental car, or public transportation from various parts of Suva or other areas in Viti Levu.

Starting Prices for Entry:

There's usually an admission fee to enter the museum, which varies depending on factors like age and nationality. Prices typically range from $5 to $10 USD.

Tips for Visiting:

- Take your time to explore the museum's various galleries and exhibits, which cover topics ranging from Fijian history and archaeology to art and culture.

Mamanuca Islands

This picturesque island group is renowned for its stunning beaches and vibrant coral reefs. While resort stays can be costly, consider budget-friendly accommodations like guesthouses or backpacker lodges. As a free alternative, hop on a day cruise that includes island hopping and snorkeling opportunities. Practical tip: Pack a reusable water bottle and snacks for the day trip. The Mamanuca Islands served as the backdrop for the reality TV show "Survivor" in several seasons.

The Mamanuca Islands are located off the western coast of Viti Levu, Fiji's main island. You can reach them by taking a ferry or boat transfer from Port Denarau or other nearby ports. Alternatively, you can book a seaplane or helicopter transfer for a more scenic journey.

Once you arrive, you'll discover a tropical paradise with pristine beaches, turquoise waters, and vibrant coral reefs. The Mamanuca Islands are renowned for their stunning natural beauty and offer a wide range of activities, including snorkeling, diving, kayaking, and island hopping.

Tips for Visiting:

- While resort stays on the Mamanuca Islands can be costly, you can save money by opting for budget-friendly accommodations like guesthouses or backpacker lodges.
- Consider booking a day cruise that includes island hopping and snorkeling opportunities as a more affordable way to explore the islands.
- Pack a reusable water bottle and snacks for the day trip to save money on refreshments.

Sigatoka Sand Dunes National Park

These impressive sand dunes along Fiji's Coral Coast offer a unique landscape to explore. While there's a small entrance fee, you can save by joining guided tours that provide insights into the area's geological and cultural significance. As a free alternative, embark on self-guided hikes along the coastal trails, where you can spot native flora and fauna. Practical tip: Wear sunscreen and a hat, as there's limited shade on the dunes. The park is believed to have been inhabited for over 2,600 years, with archaeological evidence of ancient settlements.

Sigatoka Sand Dunes National Park is located along Fiji's Coral Coast, approximately 5 kilometers (3 miles) north of Sigatoka town on the main island of Viti Levu. You can reach it by taxi, rental car, or local bus from Nadi, Suva, or other areas on Viti Levu.

Exploring the Park:

Once you arrive, you'll find yourself amidst impressive sand dunes, coastal vegetation, and stunning views of the ocean. Sigatoka Sand Dunes National Park offers opportunities for hiking, birdwatching, and learning about the area's geological and cultural significance.

Starting Prices for Entry:

There's usually an entrance fee to enter the national park, which is typically around $10 USD for adults. Prices may vary depending on factors like age and nationality.

Tips for Visiting:

- Wear sunscreen and a hat, as there's limited shade on the dunes, especially during the midday sun.

- Join guided tours offered by the park rangers to learn more about the area's natural and cultural heritage.
- Bring plenty of water and snacks, as there are limited facilities within the park.

Navua River Cruise

Embark on a scenic cruise along the Navua River, surrounded by lush rainforest and waterfalls. While cruise packages can be pricey, look for discounts by booking in groups or combining your trip with other activities like zip-lining or village visits. As a free alternative, explore the riverside villages on foot and interact with locals to learn about their traditional way of life. Practical tip: Bring a waterproof camera to capture the stunning scenery. The Navua River played a significant role in Fiji's history as a trade route for early settlers.

The Navua River Cruise typically departs from Pacific Harbour, which is located on the southern coast of Viti Levu, Fiji's main island. You can reach Pacific Harbour by taxi, rental car, or local bus from Nadi, Suva, or other areas on Viti Levu.

Exploring the River:

Once you arrive, you'll embark on a scenic cruise along the Navua River, surrounded by lush rainforest, cascading waterfalls, and traditional Fijian villages. The cruise offers opportunities for sightseeing, photography, and cultural immersion.

Tips for Visiting:

- Book your cruise in advance to secure your spot, especially during peak tourist seasons.
- Bring a waterproof camera to capture the stunning scenery along the river, including waterfalls, wildlife, and village life.

Pacific Harbour

Known as the adventure capital of Fiji, Pacific Harbour offers adrenaline-pumping activities like shark diving and zip-lining. While these experiences come with a hefty price tag, you can save by booking packages that include multiple activities or by visiting during promotional periods. As a free alternative, take a leisurely stroll along the coastal boardwalks and watch the sunset over Beqa Lagoon. Practical tip: Research operators thoroughly and ensure they adhere to safety standards. Pacific Harbour was developed in the 1970s as a planned residential and resort community.

Pacific Harbour is located on the southern coast of Viti Levu, Fiji's main island. You can reach it by taxi, rental car, or local bus from Nadi, Suva, or other areas on Viti Levu. The most common route is via the Queens Road, which runs along the southern coast of the island.

Exploring the Area:

Once you arrive, you'll discover that Pacific Harbour is known as the adventure capital of Fiji, offering a wide range of adrenaline-pumping activities. From shark diving and zip-lining to cultural experiences and nature walks, there's something for everyone in Pacific Harbour.

Tips for Visiting:

- Research operators thoroughly and ensure they adhere to safety standards, especially for adventure activities like shark diving and zip-lining.
- Consider booking package deals that include multiple activities or meals to save money on overall costs.
- Take a leisurely stroll along the coastal boardwalks and watch the sunset over Beqa Lagoon for a relaxing end to your day.

The Islands

Fiji is an archipelago of over 330 islands, each offering its own unique charm and attractions. While some islands are more popular and frequently visited by tourists, others remain relatively untouched and secluded.

The Fijian islands are grouped into tourist destination categories based on their unique geographical features, cultural characteristics, and the types of experiences they offer to visitors. Here's why each group of islands is categorized as such:

- **Mamanuca Islands:**
    - These islands are known for their stunning beaches, clear waters, and luxurious resorts, making them a popular choice for tourists seeking relaxation and indulgence.
    - The Mamanuca Islands offer a wide range of water-based activities such as snorkeling, scuba diving, sailing, and surfing, making them an ideal destination for beach lovers and water sports enthusiasts.
- **Yasawa Islands:**
    - The Yasawa Islands are characterized by rugged landscapes, remote beaches, and traditional Fijian villages, providing a more authentic and off-the-beaten-path experience compared to the Mamanucas.
    - Visitors to the Yasawas can immerse themselves in Fijian culture, explore untouched natural beauty, and engage in activities such as hiking, village visits, and cultural ceremonies.
- **Lau Group:**
    - The Lau Group comprises remote and largely untouched islands known for their pristine coral reefs, traditional culture, and unique biodiversity.
    - Access to the Lau Group is limited, but it offers incredible opportunities for adventure and exploration, including world-class diving, snorkeling, and wildlife encounters.
- **Coral Coast:**
    - Stretching along the southern coast of Viti Levu, the Coral Coast is known for its stunning coral reefs, lush rainforests, and traditional Fijian villages.
    - The Coral Coast offers a mix of luxury resorts and budget accommodations, as well as cultural experiences and outdoor activities such as hiking, horseback riding, and river safaris.
- **Pacific Harbour and Beqa Island:**
    - Pacific Harbour is known as the adventure capital of Fiji, offering a wide range of adrenaline-pumping activities such as whitewater rafting, shark diving, and zip-lining.
    - Beqa Island, located just offshore, is famous for its world-class diving sites and cultural experiences, including traditional firewalking ceremonies.

Here are the most visited islands in Fiji. We will be exploring the cheapest options to get to them, the attractions, cheapest accommodations and unmissable experiences:

- **Viti Levu**: As the main island of Fiji, Viti Levu offers budget-friendly accommodations, diverse cultural experiences, and opportunities for adventure, including hiking, waterfall visits, and cultural tours.
- **Vanua Levu**: Fiji's second-largest island, Vanua Levu, offers budget accommodations, remote beaches, and opportunities for snorkeling, diving, and exploring traditional Fijian villages.
- **Mamanuca Islands**: Known for their pristine beaches and crystal-clear waters, the Mamanuca Islands offer budget-friendly accommodations in hostels, guesthouses, and beachfront resorts, as well as opportunities for snorkeling, surfing, and island hopping.
- **Yasawa Islands**: With their rugged landscapes, secluded beaches, and budget-friendly accommodations, the Yasawa Islands are a favorite among backpackers and budget travelers seeking off-the-beaten-path experiences.
- **Taveuni**: Dubbed the "Garden Island" of Fiji, Taveuni boasts lush rainforests, cascading waterfalls, and budget-friendly accommodations, as well as opportunities for hiking, birdwatching, and exploring marine reserves.
- **Beqa Island**: Known for its vibrant coral reefs and diverse marine life, Beqa Island offers budget-friendly accommodations in beachfront resorts and guesthouses, as well as opportunities for diving, snorkeling, and cultural experiences.
- **Kadavu Island**: Offering unspoiled natural beauty and budget-friendly accommodations, Kadavu Island is a paradise for eco-conscious travelers seeking opportunities for diving, snorkeling, and exploring pristine rainforests.
- **Nacula Island**: Located in the Yasawa Islands, Nacula Island offers budget-friendly accommodations in beachfront resorts and backpacker-friendly guesthouses, as well as opportunities for snorkeling, hiking, and cultural experiences.
- **Mana Island**: With its white sandy beaches and budget-friendly accommodations, Mana Island is a popular destination for budget travelers seeking relaxation, snorkeling, and island hopping adventures.
- **Malolo Island**: Offering budget-friendly accommodations in beachfront resorts and backpacker-friendly guesthouses, Malolo Island is a favorite among budget travelers seeking opportunities for snorkeling, surfing, and cultural experiences.
- **Matamanoa Island**: Known for its secluded beaches and budget-friendly accommodations, Matamanoa Island offers opportunities for relaxation, snorkeling, and exploring nearby islands.
- **Naviti Island**: Located in the Yasawa Islands, Naviti Island offers budget-friendly accommodations in beachfront resorts and backpacker-friendly guesthouses, as well as opportunities for snorkeling, diving, and hiking.
- **Waya Island**: Offering budget-friendly accommodations in beachfront resorts and backpacker-friendly guesthouses, Waya Island is a favorite among budget travelers seeking opportunities for snorkeling, hiking, and cultural experiences.
- **Korovou Island**: Known for its budget-friendly accommodations and laid-back atmosphere, Korovou Island offers opportunities for snorkeling, diving, and exploring traditional Fijian villages.
- **Qamea Island**: Offering budget-friendly accommodations in beachfront resorts and guesthouses, Qamea Island is a paradise for budget travelers seeking opportunities for snorkeling, diving, and exploring pristine beaches.

- **Mana Island**: With its budget-friendly accommodations and vibrant coral reefs, Mana Island is a popular destination for budget travelers seeking opportunities for snorkeling, diving, and island hopping adventures.
- **Kadavu Island**: Known for its rugged landscapes and budget-friendly accommodations, Kadavu Island offers opportunities for hiking, birdwatching, and exploring traditional Fijian villages.
- **Matamanoa Island**: Offering budget-friendly accommodations in beachfront resorts and backpacker-friendly guesthouses, Matamanoa Island is a favorite among budget travelers seeking relaxation, snorkeling, and exploring nearby islands.
- **Savusavu**: Located on Vanua Levu, Savusavu offers budget-friendly accommodations, hot springs, and opportunities for snorkeling, diving, and exploring traditional Fijian villages.
- **Pacific Harbour**: Known as the adventure capital of Fiji, Pacific Harbour offers budget-friendly accommodations, adrenaline-pumping activities, and opportunities for snorkeling, diving, and exploring rainforests.

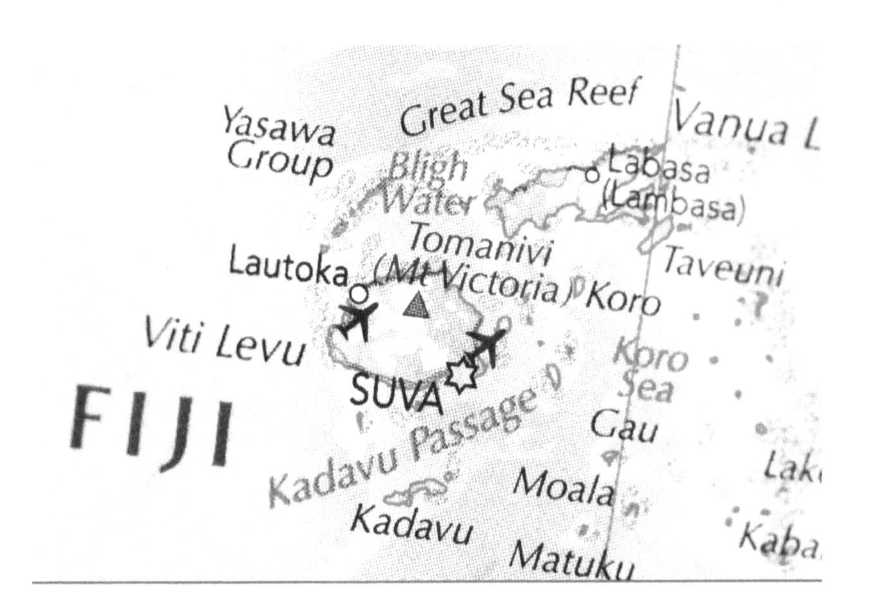
Yasawa Group
Great Sea Reef
Bligh Water
Labasa (Lambasa)
Tomanivi (Mt Victoria)
Lautoka
Taveuni
Koro
Viti Levu
Koro Sea
SUVA
FIJI
Kadavu Passage
Gau
Moala
Kadavu
Matuku

Viti Levu

Viti Levu, whose name translates to "Great Fiji," is more than just an island—it's a microcosm of Fiji's past, present, and future. Steeped in history, this island has been inhabited for thousands of years, with archaeological evidence suggesting human settlement dating back to at least 2,000 BCE. Over the centuries, Viti Levu has been shaped by waves of migration, trade, and colonization, leaving behind a rich cultural heritage that is evident in its traditions, languages, and customs.

One of the most fascinating aspects of Viti Levu's history is its role in the development of modern Fiji. It was here, in the late 18th century, that European explorers first made contact with the indigenous Fijian people, forever altering the course of the island's history. The arrival of European settlers brought profound changes to Viti Levu, including the introduction of Christianity, the establishment of sugarcane plantations, and the eventual cession of Fiji to the British Empire in 1874.

Today, traces of Viti Levu's colonial past can still be seen in its architecture, institutions, and cultural practices. From the colonial-era buildings of Suva, the bustling capital city, to the grand plantation houses scattered across the island's interior, reminders of Fiji's colonial heritage are woven into the fabric of everyday life.

But Viti Levu is more than just a repository of history—it's a living, breathing island that pulsates with energy and vitality. Its vibrant cities, such as Suva and Nadi, are hubs of commerce, culture, and innovation, where bustling markets, lively festivals, and eclectic dining scenes converge to create a kaleidoscope of experiences.

Beyond the urban centers, Viti Levu's natural beauty beckons adventurers and nature lovers alike. The island's interior is dominated by rugged mountain ranges, verdant valleys, and cascading waterfalls, offering endless opportunities for hiking, trekking, and eco-tourism. Explore the lush rainforests of Colo-i-Suva Forest Park, plunge into the refreshing waters of the Sabeto Hot Springs, or embark on a scenic drive along the Coral Coast, where pristine beaches and turquoise lagoons stretch as far as the eye can see.

And no exploration of Viti Levu would be complete without delving into its vibrant cultural tapestry. Visit traditional Fijian villages nestled in the highlands, where you can participate in kava ceremonies, witness traditional dances, and learn about age-old customs passed down through generations. Immerse yourself in the warmth and hospitality of the Fijian people, whose smiles and welcoming spirit will leave an indelible mark on your soul.

Accommodation:

- Budget Accommodation: Opt for budget-friendly guesthouses, hostels, or homestays in towns like Nadi, Suva, and Sigatoka. Prices start at around $20-30 USD per night for basic accommodations. Rendezvous Surf Camp Fiji, Nadi Bay Resort Hotel and Bluewater Lodge start at $20 and offer great bang for your buck.
- If you don't mind sharing a dorm, you can stay in 4 and 5-star resort dorms like Beachcomber Island Resort for $5.

Transportation:

- Public Buses: Utilize Fiji's public bus system for affordable transportation around Viti Levu. Fares start at around $1-2 USD per ride, making it an economical way to explore the island.
- Shared Taxis: Share taxis with other travelers for shorter distances or when traveling in groups to split the cost. Negotiate fares upfront to ensure a fair price.

Food:

- In Viti Levu, Fiji, indulging in delicious yet affordable local cuisine is a delight. Head to the bustling markets in Nadi or Suva for a taste of authentic Fijian flavors, where you can find budget-friendly delights like kokoda (Fijian ceviche), dal bhat (curry and rice), and lovo (traditional Fijian earth oven-cooked dishes) for around FJD 5 to FJD 15. Food stalls and roadside eateries offer savory treats such as roti wraps stuffed with flavorful fillings like chicken, fish, or vegetables, typically priced at FJD 3 to FJD 8. For a refreshing drink, sip on freshly squeezed tropical fruit juices or coconut water, available for around FJD 2 to FJD 5. Whether you're exploring the vibrant streets of Nadi or venturing into Suva's culinary scene, Viti Levu's cheap eats promise a tantalizing journey through Fijian gastronomy without breaking the bank.
- Markets: Shop for fresh produce, snacks, and meals at local markets like Nadi Market or Suva Municipal Market. You'll find a variety of affordable fruits, vegetables, and street food options.

Top Attractions in Viti Levu:

- **Sigatoka Sand Dunes National Park:** Explore the mesmerizing landscape of Fiji's first national park, boasting towering dunes and stunning ocean views. With a mere $5 USD entrance fee, this natural wonder provides an affordable escape into Fiji's raw beauty. Don't forget to visit during off-peak hours to relish discounted rates and the tranquility of the surroundings.
- **Suva Municipal Market:** Dive into the heart of Fijian culture at this bustling market, where vibrant stalls overflow with fresh produce and local delicacies. Admission is free, allowing you to immerse yourself in the sensory delights of Fijian cuisine without breaking the bank. Bargain with friendly vendors to snag the best deals and savor the authentic flavors of Fiji.

- **Sri Siva Subramaniya Temple (Nadi):** Delve into the spiritual heritage of Fiji at this exquisite Hindu temple, adorned with intricate carvings and vibrant colors. Entrance is free, welcoming all to explore its sacred grounds and marvel at its architectural splendor. Take advantage of free guided tours to uncover the temple's rich history and significance, offering an enriching cultural experience at no cost.
- **Kula Eco Park (Sigatoka):** Embark on a journey of discovery at this ecological sanctuary, home to diverse flora and fauna native to Fiji. While the entry fee is $20 USD, keep an eye out for discounted rates or combo packages with other attractions to maximize your savings. Wander through lush gardens, encounter endangered species, and participate in educational experiences that promote conservation efforts in Fiji.
- **Colo-I-Suva Forest Park (Suva):** Escape the hustle and bustle of city life at this verdant oasis, where lush rainforest trails lead to cascading waterfalls and crystal-clear pools. With an entry fee of $5 USD, it's an affordable retreat into nature's embrace. Bring your own snacks and drinks for a budget-friendly picnic amidst the serene beauty of Colo-I-Suva, ensuring a memorable day out without splurging on food costs.
- **Natadola Beach**:
    - Starting Price: Free (public beach)
    - Money Saving Tip: Pack your own beach gear and snacks for a budget-friendly day at the beach.
- **Navala Village**:
    - Starting Price: Free (guided tours may require a donation)
    - Respect local customs and traditions, and purchase handmade crafts directly from villagers to support the community.
- **Fiji Museum** (Suva):
    - Starting Price: $10 USD (entry fee)
    - Money Saving Tip: Check for student or senior discounts, and visit on Thursday afternoons for lower admission prices.
- **Garden of the Sleeping Giant** (Nadi):
    - Starting Price: $15 USD (entry fee)
    - Money Saving Tip: Visit during the early morning or late afternoon for cooler temperatures and fewer crowds.
- **Sabeto Hot Springs and Mud Pools** (Nadi):
    - Starting Price: $20 USD (entry fee)
    - Money Saving Tip: Bring your own towel and change of clothes to avoid rental fees.
- **Sigatoka River Safari**:
    - Starting Price: $80 USD (tour)
    - Money Saving Tip: Look for group discounts or promotional offers when booking tours on sites like **FijiBookings.com:** This website offers a variety of deals on accommodations, tours, activities, and transportation throughout Fiji. You can find discounts on everything from hotel stays to adventure tours.
- **Vuda Point Marina** (Lautoka):
    - Starting Price: Free (visit)
    - Money Saving Tip: Enjoy a leisurely stroll along the marina and watch the sunset for a budget-friendly activity.
- **Momi Bay Battery Historical Site**:
    - Starting Price: Free (entry)

    - Money Saving Tip: Pack a picnic lunch and spend the day exploring the historic site and nearby beaches.
- **Abaca Village** (Sigatoka):
    - Starting Price: Free (entry, donations welcome)
    - Money Saving Tip: Support local artisans by purchasing handmade crafts and souvenirs directly from villagers.
- **Naihehe Caves** (Sigatoka):
    - Starting Price: $10 USD (entry fee)
    - Money Saving Tip: Bring a flashlight and sturdy footwear for a self-guided exploration of the caves.
- **Sabeto Valley** (Nadi):
    - Starting Price: Free (visit)
    - Money Saving Tip: Take a self-guided hike through the valley to discover hidden waterfalls and natural swimming pools.
- **Nausori Highlands** (Suva):
    - Starting Price: Free (visit)
    - Money Saving Tip: Pack

Budget-friendly island hopping day trip options

Ferry routes from Viti Levu often include stops at popular islands such as Mana, Malolo, and Tavarua in the Mamanucas, as well as Nacula, Naviti, and Nanuya Lailai in the Yasawas.

Picture yourself standing on the bustling shores of Port Denarau, where ferries await to whisk you away. As the sun casts its golden glow upon the tranquil waters, you board a vessel bound for the Mamanuca and Yasawa Islands, a string of tropical jewels just off Viti Levu's western coast. The ferry ride itself is a scenic delight, offering panoramic views of emerald isles dotting the horizon, framed by cerulean seas that shimmer with an inviting warmth.

Prices for ferry tickets typically range from FJD 50 to FJD 150, depending on the destination, vessel, and class of service. While budget-conscious travelers may opt for standard seating, those seeking a touch of luxury can indulge in premium cabins offering comfort and convenience.

Here are some of the cheapest options to explore nearby islands:

- **Mamanuca Islands**: These picturesque islands are just a short boat ride away from the main island of Fiji. Several tour operators offer affordable day trips to various Mamanuca Islands, where you can enjoy snorkeling, swimming, and beach picnics.
- **Yasawa Islands**: Another stunning island group near Fiji's main island, the Yasawa Islands offer budget-friendly day trips with opportunities for snorkeling, exploring traditional villages, and relaxing on pristine beaches.
- **Beachcomber Island**: Known for its beautiful beaches and vibrant coral reefs, Beachcomber Island is a popular day trip destination from Fiji's main island. You can find reasonably priced boat transfers and day tour packages to explore this tropical paradise.
- **Cloud 9 Floating Platform**: If you're looking for a unique experience, consider a day trip to Cloud 9, a floating platform located in the crystal-clear waters of the Pacific Ocean. You can relax on sun loungers, enjoy drinks at the bar, and even try water sports like snorkeling and paddleboarding.
- **Tivua Island**: Tivua Island offers a secluded and peaceful retreat just a short boat ride from the main island. Day trips often include activities like snorkeling, kayaking, and traditional Fijian entertainment, making it a great value for budget-conscious travelers.
- **Viti Levu's Coral Coast**: Explore the Coral Coast of Viti Levu, Fiji's main island, on a budget-friendly day trip. Visit scenic spots like Sigatoka Sand Dunes National Park, Natadola Beach, and the Sigatoka River for an affordable and memorable experience.
- **Navua River**: Take a day trip to the Navua River for an adventurous journey through Fiji's lush interior. Many tour operators offer affordable river rafting trips and cultural experiences along the Navua River, allowing you to immerse yourself in Fiji's natural beauty.

Pacific Harbour

Nestled along the southeastern coast of Viti Levu, Fiji's main island, lies the idyllic town of Pacific Harbour, a haven for adventure seekers, nature lovers, and those seeking a slice of Fijian paradise. Known as the "Adventure Capital of Fiji," Pacific Harbour offers a perfect blend of adrenaline-pumping activities, pristine nature, and warm Fijian hospitality. Join us as we explore the enchanting allure of Pacific Harbour and uncover its many treasures.

Pacific Harbour's stunning coastal location provides a picturesque backdrop for a wide range of outdoor adventures. The town is renowned for its world-class diving and snorkeling sites, including the iconic Beqa Lagoon, home to vibrant coral reefs, colorful marine life, and thrilling shark dives. Dive into the crystal-clear waters and swim alongside reef sharks, manta rays, and other fascinating creatures, or explore the underwater caves and shipwrecks that dot the ocean floor.

But Pacific Harbour is not just a destination for water sports—it's also a playground for land-based adventures and cultural experiences. Embark on guided tours through the lush rainforests of the surrounding highlands, where you can hike to hidden waterfalls, zipline through the canopy, or trek to remote villages to learn about traditional Fijian culture and customs. Visit the nearby Arts Village, where you can browse local handicrafts, watch traditional Fijian performances, and sample delicious Fijian cuisine at the village's restaurants and cafes.

For adrenaline junkies, Pacific Harbour offers a range of thrilling activities guaranteed to get your heart racing. Experience the rush of whitewater rafting on the nearby Navua River, where you can navigate rapids, swim in natural pools, and admire the stunning scenery of lush tropical forests and cascading waterfalls. Take on the challenge of off-road quad biking through rugged terrain, or soar through the skies on a breathtaking helicopter tour, offering panoramic views of Fiji's stunning landscapes from above.

After a day of adventure, unwind and relax in Pacific Harbour's laid-back atmosphere, where you can stroll along the waterfront promenade, savor fresh seafood at waterfront restaurants, or simply watch the sunset over the horizon. With its warm climate, friendly locals, and stunning natural beauty, Pacific Harbour offers the perfect escape for those seeking adventure, relaxation, and unforgettable experiences in the heart of Fiji.

Getting to Pacific Harbour on a Budget:

Pacific Harbour is easily accessible from major cities in Fiji. Here's the most cost-effective way to reach Pacific Harbour:

- **Bus from Suva or Nadi**:
  - Buses operate regularly from Suva and Nadi to Pacific Harbour, providing a convenient and affordable mode of transportation.
  - Prices: Bus fares typically range from $5 - $15 USD per person, depending on the distance and route.
- **Shared Shuttle Service**:
  - Shared shuttle services are available from Nadi International Airport or Suva's Nausori International Airport to Pacific Harbour.
  - Prices: Shared shuttle fares start at around $20 - $30 USD per person, depending on the provider and availability.

Affordable Accommodation Options:

While Pacific Harbour offers luxury resorts, there are budget-friendly accommodations suitable for the thrifty traveler:

- **Uprising Beach Resort**: While not strictly a backpacker hostel, Uprising Beach Resort offers budget-friendly dormitory rooms alongside private bures and villas. Dormitory prices start at around $30 USD per night.
- **The Beachouse**: Located a short drive from Pacific Harbour, The Beachouse offers affordable dormitory accommodation in a relaxed beachfront setting. Dormitory prices start at around $20 USD per night.
- **Mango Bay Resort**: Situated in nearby Namatakula, Mango Bay Resort provides backpacker-style dormitory rooms alongside beachfront bures. Dormitory prices start at around $25 USD per night.
- **Namuana Hostel**: This cozy hostel in Pacific Harbour offers dormitory rooms with shared facilities. Dormitory prices start at around $15 USD per night.
- **Rivers Fiji Backpacker Camp**: Ideal for adventurous travelers, Rivers Fiji Backpacker Camp provides basic accommodation in safari tents along the Navua River. Prices start at around $20 USD per night.

- **Club Oceanus Resort**: Offering dormitory-style accommodation with shared facilities, Club Oceanus Resort is situated close to Pacific Harbour's main attractions. Dormitory prices start at around $20 USD per night.
- **Nanuku Auberge Resort**: While Nanuku Auberge Resort is a luxury property, it occasionally offers discounted rates for backpackers and budget travelers. It's worth checking their website or contacting them directly for current prices.

Vanua Levu

As the second-largest island in Fiji, Vanua Levu offers a captivating blend of lush rainforests, pristine beaches, and traditional Fijian villages, making it a haven for nature enthusiasts and cultural explorers alike. Join us as we embark on a journey to uncover the wonders and secrets of this enchanting island.

Vanua Levu, whose name translates to "Big Land" in Fijian, is a land of contrasts and diversity. Its rugged interior is cloaked in dense rainforests, home to a myriad of endemic species and cascading waterfalls that tumble down verdant slopes. Along the coast, powdery white beaches meet crystal-clear waters teeming with colorful coral reefs and marine life, offering endless opportunities for snorkeling, diving, and beachcombing.

But beyond its natural beauty, Vanua Levu is steeped in history and culture, with a rich tapestry of traditions passed down through generations. The island has been inhabited for thousands of years, with evidence of human settlement dating back to ancient times. Over the centuries, Vanua Levu has been shaped by waves of migration, trade, and colonization, resulting in a diverse cultural landscape that reflects the island's multicultural heritage.

One of the most intriguing aspects of Vanua Levu's history is its role in the development of Fiji's colonial past. European explorers first made contact with the indigenous Fijian people on the shores of Vanua Levu in the late 18th century, marking the beginning of a new chapter in the island's history. The arrival of European settlers brought significant changes to Vanua Levu, including the establishment of sugarcane plantations, the introduction of Christianity, and the eventual cession of Fiji to the British Empire in 1874.

Today, traces of Vanua Levu's colonial past can still be seen in its architecture, institutions, and cultural practices. From the colonial-era buildings of Labasa, the bustling main town, to the grand plantation houses scattered across the island's interior, reminders of Fiji's colonial heritage are woven into the fabric of everyday life.

Explore the lush rainforests of Waisali Nature Reserve, where hiking trails lead to hidden waterfalls and panoramic viewpoints. Dive into the crystal-clear waters of Savusavu Bay, where vibrant coral reefs and underwater caves await exploration. And immerse yourself in the warmth and hospitality of the Fijian people, whose smiles and welcoming spirit will leave an indelible mark on your soul.

Accommodation:

- Budget Accommodation: Look for affordable guesthouses, backpacker hostels, or homestays in towns like Savusavu and Labasa. Prices start at around $20-30 USD per night for basic accommodations.
- **Dolphin Bay Divers Retreat**: Located in the heart of Natewa Bay, this eco-friendly retreat offers budget-friendly accommodation options such as dormitories and private rooms. Prices start around $30 USD per night for a dorm bed.
- **Korovesi Sunshine Villas**: These self-contained villas offer beautiful ocean views and are located just a short drive from Savusavu town. Prices start around $80 USD per night for a studio villa.

Transportation:

- Public Buses: Utilize Fiji's public bus system for affordable transportation around Vanua Levu. Fares start at around $1-2 USD per ride, making it an economical way to explore the island.

Food:

- Markets: Shop for fresh produce, snacks, and meals at local markets like Labasa Market or Savusavu Market. You'll find a variety of affordable fruits, vegetables, and street food options. Fresh tropical fruits, seafood, and local snacks like cassava chips or fried plantains. *Price range*: $1 - $5 USD depending on the item.
- **Roadside Stalls**:
  - *What to eat*: Roti parcels filled with curry, grilled fish, or barbecued meats served with rice or roti.
  - *Price range*: $2 - $8 USD per item.
- **Fijian Cafés**:
  - *What to eat*: Fijian-style curry with rice or dhal, lovo (earth oven) cooked dishes, fish and chips.
  - *Price range*: $5 - $10 USD per meal.
- **Street Food Vendors**:
  - *What to eat*: Samosas, fried noodles, fish cakes, or coconut buns.
  - *Price range*: $1 - $5 USD per item.

- **Local Bakeries**:
    - *What to eat*: Freshly baked bread, coconut buns, pineapple turnovers, or custard tarts.
    - *Price range*: $1 - $3 USD per item.
- **Village Eateries**:
    - *What to eat*: Traditional Fijian meals like kokoda (marinated raw fish), palusami (taro leaves cooked in coconut cream), or rourou (Fijian spinach).
    - *Price range*: $5 - $10 USD per meal.
- **Fish Markets**:
    - *What to eat*: Grilled or fried fish, seafood curry, or fish kokoda.
    - *Price range*: $5 - $15 USD depending on the type and size of the fish.
- **Local Diners**:
    - *What to eat*: Roti wraps filled with chicken or beef curry, fried rice or noodles, or mixed vegetable curry with rice.
    - *Price range*: $5 - $10 USD per meal.
- **Beachside Barbecue Stands**:
    - *What to eat*: Grilled seafood skewers, fish burgers, or BBQ chicken served with salads.
    - *Price range*: $5 - $15 USD per meal.

Top Attractions in Vanua Levu:

- **Savusavu Hot Springs**:
    - Starting Price: $25 entry (visit)
    - Money Saving Tip: Bring your own towel and swimwear to enjoy a rejuvenating soak in the natural hot springs.
- **Labasa Market**:
    - Starting Price: Free (entry).
    - Money Saving Tip: Shop for fresh produce, spices, and local snacks at affordable prices, and don't forget to bargain with vendors for discounts.
- **Jean-Michel Cousteau Resort Beach** (Savusavu):
    - Starting Price: Free (beach access)
    - Money Saving Tip: Pack a picnic lunch and spend the day relaxing on the pristine white sands of this beautiful beach.
- **Nasekawa River** (Labasa):
    - Starting Price: Free (visit)
    - Money Saving Tip: Explore the scenic Nasekawa River on foot or by kayak for a budget-friendly outdoor adventure.
- **Waisali Rainforest Reserve**:
    - Starting Price: $10 USD (entry fee)
    - Money Saving Tip: Bring your own water and snacks for a self-guided hike through the lush rainforest, and keep an eye out for native wildlife.
- **Dolphin Bay Divers Retreat** (Taveuni):
    - Starting Price: Free (visit)
    - Money Saving Tip: Enjoy snorkeling or diving in the nearby reef for an affordable underwater adventure.
- **Vatu-i-Ra Conservation Park**:
    - Starting Price: Free (visit)
    - Money Saving Tip: Explore the marine reserve's vibrant coral reefs and diverse marine life by snorkeling or kayaking for a budget-friendly aquatic experience.
- **Korolevu Beach** (Nabouwalu):

- Starting Price: Free (beach access)
    - Money Saving Tip: Bring your own beach gear and snacks for a relaxing day by the sea, and watch the sunset over the horizon.
- **Vuadomo Village** (Labasa):
    - Starting Price: Free (visit, donations welcome)
    - Money Saving Tip: Participate in a traditional kava ceremony or meke performance to experience Fijian culture firsthand.
- **Wasavula Village** (Savusavu):
    - Starting Price: Free (visit, donations welcome)
    - Money Saving Tip: Support local artisans by purchasing handmade crafts and souvenirs directly from villagers.
- **Nakawaga Waterfall** (Nabouwalu):
    - Starting Price: Free (visit)
    - Money Saving Tip: Take a scenic hike to the waterfall and enjoy a refreshing swim in the natural pool at the base.
- **Nasavusavu Beach** (Savusavu):
    - Starting Price: Free (beach access)
    - Money Saving Tip: Pack a picnic lunch and spend the day lounging on the sandy shores of this secluded beach.
- **Nadogo Village** (Labasa):
    - Starting Price: Free (visit, donations welcome)
    - Money Saving Tip: Learn about traditional Fijian customs and practices during a guided tour of the village.
- **Waitavala Water Slide** (Taveuni):
    - Starting Price: $10 USD (entry fee)
    - Money Saving Tip: Bring your own inflatable tube for a thrilling ride down the natural waterslide, and enjoy the surrounding rainforest scenery.
- **Bukuya Village** (Nabouwalu):
    - Starting Price: Free (visit, donations welcome)
    - Money Saving Tip: Participate in a Fijian cooking class or craft-making workshop for an interactive cultural experience.
- **Sesevu Village** (Savusavu):
    - Starting Price: Free (visit, donations welcome)

Denarau Island

Renowned for its upscale accommodations, championship golf courses, and vibrant marina, Denarau Island beckons travelers seeking a slice of paradise with a touch of sophistication. Join us as we explore the allure and elegance of this exclusive island retreat.

Denarau Island, whose name translates to "Island of Dreams" in Fijian, lives up to its moniker with its picture-perfect landscapes and idyllic setting. Originally a mangrove swamp, the island was transformed into a premier tourist destination through a series of ambitious development projects in the late 20th century. Today, Denarau Island stands as a testament to the vision and ingenuity of its developers, offering an unparalleled blend of luxury, comfort, and natural beauty.

One of the most striking features of Denarau Island is its collection of world-class resorts and hotels, which cater to the discerning tastes of luxury travelers from around the globe. From five-star beachfront villas to lavish suites with panoramic ocean views, accommodations on Denarau Island are designed to pamper and indulge, offering a sanctuary of serenity and relaxation.

But Denarau Island is more than just a haven for luxury travelers—it's also a playground for adventure seekers and outdoor enthusiasts. Tee off at the renowned Denarau Golf and Racquet Club, where immaculately manicured fairways and challenging courses await golfers of all skill levels. Set sail on a scenic cruise around the nearby Mamanuca and Yasawa Islands, where secluded beaches, hidden coves, and vibrant coral reefs beckon snorkelers, divers, and sun worshippers alike.

And no visit to Denarau Island would be complete without a stroll along the bustling marina, where luxury yachts, sailboats, and catamarans bob gently in the turquoise waters of the Pacific Ocean. Take in the sights and sounds of this vibrant waterfront promenade, where shops, cafes, and boutiques beckon with their tantalizing offerings.

Accommodation:

- Budget Accommodation: While Denarau Island is known for its luxury resorts, you can still find budget-friendly accommodations by booking in advance or opting for smaller hotels or guesthouses. Here are two guesthouses in Denarau Island along with approximate prices:
- **Wailoaloa Beach Resort Fiji**:
    - This resort offers budget-friendly accommodation options including dormitory beds and private rooms.
    - Prices: Dormitory beds start around $25 - $30 USD per night, while private rooms start around $60 - $80 USD per night.
    - Location: Wailoaloa Beach Road, Nadi, Fiji (about a 20-minute drive from Denarau Island).
- **Smugglers Cove Beach Resort & Hotel**:
    - While not exactly a guesthouse, Smugglers Cove offers affordable accommodations including dormitory beds and private rooms.
    - Prices: Dormitory beds start around $30 - $40 USD per night, while private rooms start around $80 - $100 USD per night.
    - Location: Wailoaloa Beach Road, Nadi, Fiji (about a 20-minute drive from Denarau Island).

Transportation:

- Public Buses: Utilize Fiji's public bus system to travel between Denarau Island and nearby towns like Nadi or Lautoka. Fares are affordable, typically ranging from $1-2 USD per ride.

Food:

- Dining Options: While dining at the resort restaurants on Denarau Island can be expensive, you can find more budget-friendly dining options at shopping centers or in Nadi Town. Look for local eateries or food courts for affordable meals.

Top Attractions in Denarau Island:

- **Port Denarau Marina**:
    - Starting Price: Free (visit)
    - Money Saving Tip: Explore the marina and enjoy views of luxury yachts and boats without spending a penny.
- **Denarau Golf and Racquet Club**:
    - Starting Price: $50 USD (golf)
    - Money Saving Tip: Play a round of golf during twilight hours for discounted rates.
- **Denarau Island Beaches**:
    - Starting Price: Free (beach access)

- Money Saving Tip: Pack your own beach gear and snacks for a budget-friendly day at the beach.
- **Island-Hopping Tours**:
  - Starting Price: $50-100 USD (half-day tour)
  - Money Saving Tip: Look for group discounts or book tours directly through tour operators for better deals.
- **Cultural Performances at Resorts**:
  - Starting Price: Free (some resorts offer complimentary cultural shows)
  - Money Saving Tip: Check with your resort for free or discounted cultural performances during your stay.
- **Shopping at Port Denarau**:
  - Starting Price: Free to browse
  - Money Saving Tip: Window shop and enjoy the atmosphere without feeling pressured to make purchases.

Mamanuca Islands

The Mamanuca Islands, a stunning archipelago of over 20 islands, are located just off the western coast of Viti Levu, Fiji's main island. Named after a Fijian chief who once ruled the region, the Mamanuca Islands are known for their picture-perfect landscapes, with powdery white beaches, swaying palm trees, and crystal-clear waters stretching as far as the eye can see. Each island in the group boasts its own unique charm and character, from the bustling resorts of Malolo Island to the secluded hideaways of Tavarua and Monuriki.

One of the most striking features of the Mamanuca Islands is their vibrant coral reefs, which teem with a kaleidoscope of marine life. Snorkelers and divers flock to the islands to explore these underwater wonderlands, where colorful fish, sea turtles, and vibrant corals abound. Dive sites such as the famous "Cloudbreak" offer world-class reef breaks and exhilarating surf conditions, attracting surfers from around the globe seeking the ultimate wave.

But the Mamanuca Islands are not just for adrenaline junkies—they're also a haven for relaxation and rejuvenation. Luxury resorts and boutique hotels dot the islands' shores, offering an array of amenities and activities designed to pamper and indulge. From beachfront villas with private plunge pools to overwater bungalows with uninterrupted ocean views, accommodations in the Mamanuca Islands are the epitome of tropical luxury.

For those seeking a taste of Fijian culture and tradition, the Mamanuca Islands offer opportunities to connect with the local community and learn about the islands' rich heritage. Visit traditional Fijian villages on the islands of Yanuya and Malolo, where you can participate in kava ceremonies, witness traditional dances, and learn about age-old customs passed down through generations. Sample delicious Fijian cuisine at one of the islands' gourmet restaurants, where fresh seafood, tropical fruits, and exotic spices combine to create an unforgettable dining experience.

And no visit to the Mamanuca Islands would be complete without a sunset cruise around the archipelago, where you can toast to another day in paradise as the sky explodes in a riot of colors. Watch as the sun dips below the horizon, casting a golden glow over the tranquil waters and painting the clouds in shades of pink, orange, and purple—a fitting end to a day of adventure and relaxation in this tropical paradise.

Island hopping within Mamanuca Islands

Island hopping around the Mamanuca Islands can be an exciting and budget-friendly adventure. Here's a guide to the cheapest methods, starting prices, and tips to save money:

- **Public Ferry Services:**
    - **Starting Prices:** Public ferry services, such as the South Sea Cruises, offer affordable options for island hopping in the Mamanuca Islands. Prices for a one-way ticket typically start at around $20 - $30 USD per person, depending on the route and destination.
        - **Tips to Save:**
        - Book tickets in advance to secure lower fares and avoid peak travel times.
        - Pack light as excess luggage may incur additional fees.
- **Water Taxis:**
    - **Starting Prices:** Water taxis provide a flexible and cost-effective way to hop between islands in the Mamanucas. Prices vary depending on the distance traveled, but expect starting prices of around $50 - $100 USD per trip for a group.
        - **Tips to Save:**
        - Travel with a group to split the cost of the water taxi fare.
        - Negotiate prices with water taxi operators, especially if traveling during off-peak times or booking multiple trips.
- **Budget Accommodations with Transfers:**
    - **Starting Prices:** Many budget-friendly accommodations in the Mamanuca Islands offer complimentary or discounted transfers between islands as part of their stay packages.

Accommodation:

The Mamanuca Islands are primarily known for their luxurious resorts and beachfront hotels, so finding truly budget-friendly guesthouses can be quite challenging. However, there are a few options available for travelers seeking more affordable accommodations. Here are a couple of options:

Beachcomber Island Resort:

- **Description:** Beachcomber Island Resort is a popular budget-friendly accommodation located on its private island in the Mamanucas. The resort offers dormitory-style accommodations and traditional beachfront bures at affordable rates.
- **Transfers:** Beachcomber Island Resort provides daily transfers from Port Denarau via the Beachcomber Island ferry. The ferry ride takes approximately 45 minutes and is included in the accommodation package.
- **Starting Prices:** Prices for dormitory beds start at around $50 USD per person per night, while private bures start at around $100 USD per night.
- **Barefoot Manta Island**:
    - This eco-resort offers budget-friendly accommodation options in traditional Fijian bures (bungalows) and dormitories.
    - Prices: Dormitory beds start around $50 - $60 USD per night, while private bures start around $100 - $150 USD per night.
    - Location: Drawaqa Island, Mamanuca Islands,.
- **South Sea Island**:
    - This small island resort offers basic accommodation options including dormitory beds and beachfront bures.
    - Prices: Dormitory beds start around $60 - $70 USD per night, while private bures start around $150 - $200 USD per night.
    - Location: South Sea Island, Mamanuca Islands.

Transportation:

- Ferry Services: Utilize ferry services from Port Denarau in Nadi to reach the Mamanuca Islands. Look for budget-friendly ferry options or book round-trip tickets in advance for discounted rates.
- Day Trips: Instead of staying overnight on the Mamanuca Islands, consider booking day trips from Nadi or Denarau for a more budget-friendly option.

Food:

- Dining Options: While dining at the resort restaurants on the Mamanuca Islands can be expensive, you can find more budget-friendly dining options at nearby shopping centers or in Nadi Town. Look for local eateries or food courts for affordable meals.
- Self-Catering: Consider staying at accommodations with kitchen facilities or bringing your own snacks and drinks to save on dining expenses.

Activities:

- Free Attractions: Many resorts offer free access to their beaches, where you can swim, sunbathe, or enjoy water sports like snorkeling or kayaking.
- Discounted Activities: Look for discounted packages or promotions for activities like boat tours, snorkeling trips, or island hopping. Many tour operators offer special deals for guests staying in nearby areas like Nadi or Denarau.

Top Attractions in the Mamanuca Islands:

- **Snorkeling and Diving**:
  - Starting Price: $50-100 USD (half-day tour)
  - Money Saving Tip: Bring your own snorkeling gear to save on rental fees, or book tours directly through tour operators for better deals.
- **Island Hopping**:
  - Starting Price: $50-100 USD (half-day tour)
  - Money Saving Tip: Look for group discounts or book tours in advance for better rates.
- **Sunset Cruises**:
  - Starting Price: $50-100 USD (sunset cruise)
  - Money Saving Tip: Opt for shared sunset cruises to split the cost with other travelers.
- **Water Sports Rentals**:
  - Starting Price: $20-50 USD (per hour)
  - Money Saving Tip: Look for resorts offering complimentary water sports equipment for guests.
- **Coral Reefs**:
  - Starting Price: Free (snorkeling)
  - Money Saving Tip: Bring your own snorkeling gear or rent from local shops for a budget-friendly underwater adventure.
- **Beach Volleyball**:
  - Starting Price: Free (beach access)
  - Money Saving Tip: Join in on pickup games with other travelers for free entertainment.
- **Beach Picnics**:
  - Starting Price: Free to bring your own food
  - Money Saving Tip: Pack a picnic lunch and enjoy a beachfront meal without restaurant prices.
- **Coconut Grove**:
  - Starting Price: Free (visit)
  - Money Saving Tip: Enjoy a leisurely stroll through Coconut Grove's lush gardens without spending a dime.
- **Island Walks**:
  - Starting Price: Free (walk)
  - Money Saving Tip: Explore the islands on foot for a budget-friendly way to experience their natural beauty.
- **Sunbathing**:
  - Starting Price: Free (beach access)
  - Money Saving Tip: Bring your own beach towel and sunscreen to avoid purchasing them at resort prices.
- **Beach Yoga**:
  - Starting Price: Free (group sessions)

    - Money Saving Tip: Join in on group yoga sessions offered by resorts for a free fitness activity.
- **Island Barbecues**:
    - Starting Price: Free (public barbecue areas)
    - Money Saving Tip: Use public barbecue facilities to cook your own meals and enjoy a beachfront picnic.

Mana Island

One of the most alluring features of Mana Island is its pristine beaches, which offer the perfect setting for relaxation and rejuvenation. Whether you're lounging beneath the shade of a palm tree, strolling along the shoreline at sunset, or indulging in water sports such as kayaking and paddleboarding, Mana's beaches provide endless opportunities for blissful moments by the sea.

But Mana Island is not just a sanctuary for beach lovers—it's also a paradise for adventure seekers and outdoor enthusiasts. Embark on hiking trails that wind through the island's lush interior, offering panoramic views of the surrounding ocean and neighboring islands. Explore hidden caves, ancient archaeological sites, and secluded lagoons tucked away amidst the island's rugged terrain.

For those seeking a taste of Fijian culture and tradition, Mana Island offers opportunities to connect with the local community and learn about the island's rich heritage. Visit traditional Fijian villages where you can participate in kava ceremonies, witness traditional dances, and learn about age-old customs and traditions passed down through generations. Sample delicious Fijian cuisine at one of the island's restaurants, where fresh seafood, tropical fruits, and indigenous spices combine to create a culinary experience like no other.

Affordable Accommodation Options:

- **Mana Lagoon Backpackers**:
- Mana Lagoon Backpackers offers budget-friendly accommodation options including dormitory beds and basic bures (bungalows).
- Prices: Dormitory beds start at around $30 - $40 USD per night, while basic bures start at around $70 - $80 USD per night.

- Enjoy access to the hostel's amenities and activities, including snorkeling, kayaking, and beach volleyball.

Malolo Island

Malolo Island, located in the heart of the Mamanuca archipelago, is renowned for its breathtaking natural beauty and serene ambiance. The island boasts powdery white sands caressed by gentle ocean breezes, while its interior is adorned with verdant hillsides and swaying coconut palms. Surrounded by vibrant coral reefs teeming with marine life, Malolo offers endless opportunities for snorkeling, diving, and water sports, making it a haven for outdoor enthusiasts and beach lovers alike.

For those seeking a taste of Fijian culture and tradition, Malolo Island offers opportunities to connect with the local community and learn about the island's rich heritage. Visit traditional Fijian villages where you can participate in kava ceremonies, witness traditional dances, and learn about age-old customs and traditions passed down through generations. Sample delicious Fijian cuisine at one of the island's restaurants, where fresh seafood, tropical fruits, and indigenous spices combine to create a culinary experience like no other.

And no visit to Malolo Island would be complete without exploring its underwater wonders. Dive into the crystal-clear waters and discover vibrant coral gardens, underwater caves, and an array of marine life, including colorful fish, sea turtles, and reef sharks. Whether you're an experienced diver or a novice snorkeler, Malolo's reefs offer an unforgettable glimpse into the beauty of the underwater world.

Getting to Malolo Island on a Budget:

Malolo Island is accessible by boat or ferry from Viti Levu. Here's the most cost-effective way to reach Malolo Island:

- **Ferry from Port Denarau**:

- South Sea Cruises and other ferry companies operate regular services from Port Denarau on Viti Levu to Malolo Island.
- Prices: Ferry tickets typically cost around $50 - $70 USD per person for a one-way trip, depending on the season and availability.
- Book your ferry tickets in advance to secure your spot, especially during peak travel seasons.

Matamanoa Island

Matamanoa Island, located in the heart of the Mamanuca Islands, is renowned for its breathtaking vistas, powdery white sands, and crystal-clear waters teeming with marine life. The island's rugged coastline is dotted with secluded beaches and hidden coves, providing the perfect backdrop for romantic strolls, leisurely sunbathing, and unforgettable sunsets. Surrounded by vibrant coral reefs, Matamanoa offers world-class snorkeling and diving opportunities, inviting visitors to explore its underwater wonders.

One of the most captivating features of Matamanoa Island is its serene ambiance and sense of seclusion. With no roads or cars on the island, Matamanoa offers a true escape from the hustle and bustle of everyday life, allowing visitors to reconnect with nature and themselves. Whether you're unwinding in a hammock beneath the shade of a palm tree, indulging in a spa treatment overlooking the ocean, or enjoying a romantic dinner on the beach, Matamanoa offers moments of pure bliss and relaxation.

But Matamanoa Island is not just a retreat for relaxation—it's also a playground for adventure seekers and cultural enthusiasts. Embark on guided hikes through the island's lush interior, where you can discover hidden waterfalls, ancient archaeological sites, and panoramic viewpoints offering sweeping vistas of the surrounding ocean. Explore nearby uninhabited islands on a kayak or paddleboard, or join a guided snorkeling tour to explore the colorful coral reefs and underwater caves that surround Matamanoa.

For those seeking a taste of Fijian culture and tradition, Matamanoa Island offers opportunities to connect with the local community and learn about the island's rich heritage. Participate in traditional Fijian ceremonies such as kava drinking, meke dancing, and lovo feasting, where you can immerse yourself in the warmth and hospitality of the Fijian people. Sample delicious Fijian cuisine at one of the island's restaurants, where fresh seafood, tropical fruits, and indigenous spices combine to create a culinary experience like no other.

And no visit to Matamanoa Island would be complete without exploring its underwater wonders. Dive into the crystal-clear waters and discover vibrant coral gardens, underwater caves, and an array of marine life, including colorful fish, sea turtles, and reef sharks. Whether you're an experienced diver or a novice snorkeler, Matamanoa's reefs offer an unforgettable glimpse into the beauty of the underwater world.

Getting to Matamanoa Island on a Budget:

Matamanoa Island is accessible by boat or ferry from Viti Levu. Here's the most cost-effective way to reach Matamanoa Island:

- **Ferry from Port Denarau**:
- South Sea Cruises and other ferry companies operate regular services from Port Denarau on Viti Levu to Matamanoa Island.
- Prices: Ferry tickets typically cost around $50 - $70 USD per person for a one-way trip, depending on the season and availability.
- Book your ferry tickets in advance to secure your spot, especially during peak travel seasons.

Yasawa Islands

If you seek a refuge from the chaos of the world, a sanctuary for the soul, then look no further than the Yasawa Islands. For here, in this corner of paradise, you will find not just a destination, but an experience – an invitation to embrace the beauty of the natural world and the boundless depths of the human spirit.

Stretching northwest from the main island of Viti Levu, the Yasawa Islands comprise a chain of 20 volcanic islands, each more stunning than the last. Named after a Fijian word meaning "heaven," the Yasawas are renowned for their dramatic cliffs, powdery white beaches, and crystal-clear waters teeming with marine life. From the rugged peaks of Waya Island to the secluded coves of Nanuya Lailai, each island in the group boasts its own unique beauty and charm, waiting to be explored.

One of the most captivating features of the Yasawa Islands is their rich cultural heritage, which dates back thousands of years. Traditionally inhabited by the indigenous Fijian people, the islands are home to a vibrant community that maintains age-old customs and traditions. Visitors to the Yasawas have the opportunity to immerse themselves in Fijian culture, participating in kava ceremonies, witnessing traditional dances, and learning about the islands' fascinating history from local guides.

But the Yasawa Islands are not just for cultural immersion—they're also a paradise for outdoor enthusiasts and adventure seekers. Hiking trails crisscross the islands, leading to panoramic viewpoints, hidden waterfalls, and lush rainforests teeming with endemic flora and fauna. Snorkelers and divers are drawn to the Yasawas' vibrant coral reefs, where they can swim alongside colorful fish, sea turtles, and reef sharks in waters of unparalleled clarity.

For those seeking a taste of luxury and indulgence, the Yasawa Islands offer a range of upscale resorts and boutique hotels, each offering a unique blend of comfort and sophistication.

And no visit to the Yasawa Islands would be complete without experiencing a traditional Fijian lovo feast, where succulent meats, fresh seafood, and tropical fruits are cooked underground in an earth oven, imbuing them with smoky flavor and tender juiciness.

Getting there

The most affordable option for traveling to the Yasawa Islands is by using ferry services operated by either Awesome Adventures Fiji or South Sea Cruises. These ferries depart from Port Denarau in Nadi. Ferry tickets start at around $100 - $150 USD per person for a one-way trip, depending on the destination within the Yasawa Islands and the class of service. Book in advance for discounts.

Island hopping between Yasawa Islands

The cheapest way to get between the islands is to stay somewhere with free transfers. Here are some options for affordable island hopping in the Yasawas:

- **Blue Lagoon Beach Resort:**
  - **Description:** Blue Lagoon Beach Resort is a popular budget-friendly accommodation located on Nacula Island in the Yasawas. The resort offers traditional beachfront bures and dormitory-style accommodations.
  - **Transfers:** Blue Lagoon Beach Resort provides complimentary transfers from Denarau Marina on Viti Levu to the resort via the Yasawa Flyer ferry. The transfer is included in the accommodation package.
  - **Starting Prices:** Prices for dormitory beds start at around $40 USD per person per night, while beachfront bures start at around $100 USD per night.
- **Oarsman's Bay Lodge:**
  - **Description:** Oarsman's Bay Lodge is a budget-friendly accommodation located on Nacula Island. The lodge offers traditional Fijian bures and beachfront tents at affordable rates.
  - **Transfers:** Oarsman's Bay Lodge provides complimentary transfers from Denarau Marina to the resort via the Yasawa Flyer ferry. The transfer is included in the accommodation package.
  - **Starting Prices:** Prices for beachfront tents start at around $60 USD per person per night, while traditional bures start at around $100 USD per night.
- **Gold Coast Resort:**
  - **Description:** Gold Coast Resort is a budget-friendly accommodation located on Nanuya Lailai Island in the Yasawas. The resort offers traditional beachfront bures and dormitory-style accommodations.
  - **Transfers:** Gold Coast Resort provides complimentary transfers from Denarau Marina to the resort via the Yasawa Flyer ferry. The transfer is included in the accommodation package.

- **Starting Prices:** Prices for dormitory beds start at around $30 USD per person per night, while beachfront bures start at around $80 USD per night.
- **Nanuya Island Resort:**
    - **Description:** Nanuya Island Resort is a budget-friendly accommodation located on Nanuya Lailai Island. The resort offers beachfront bures and private rooms with shared facilities.
    - **Transfers:** Nanuya Island Resort provides complimentary transfers from Denarau Marina to the resort via the Yasawa Flyer ferry. The transfer is included in the accommodation package.
    - **Starting Prices:** Prices for private rooms start at around $70 USD per night, while beachfront bures start at around $120 USD per night.

Accommodation

While the Yasawa Islands are also dominated by upscale resorts, there are a few budget-friendly guesthouses and backpacker accommodations available. Here are some options:

- **Octopus Resort**:
    - Octopus Resort offers budget-friendly accommodation options including dormitory beds and private bures.
    - Prices: Dormitory beds start around $50 - $60 USD per night, while private bures start around $150 - $200 USD per night.
    - Location: Waya Island, Yasawa Islands, Fiji.
- **Blue Lagoon Beach Resort**:
    - This resort offers a range of accommodation options including dormitories, beachfront bures, and garden bures.
    - Prices: Dormitory beds start around $50 - $60 USD per night, while private bures start around $150 - $200 USD per night.
    - Location: Nacula Island, Yasawa Islands, Fiji.
- **Gold Coast Resort**:
    - Gold Coast Resort offers budget-friendly accommodation options including dormitory beds and private bures.
    - Prices: Dormitory beds start around $50 - $60 USD per night, while private bures start around $150 - $200 USD per night.
    - Location: Waya Island, Yasawa Islands, Fiji.
- **Barefoot Manta Island**:
    - As mentioned earlier, Barefoot Manta Island offers budget-friendly accommodation options including dormitory beds and private bures.
    - Prices: Dormitory beds start around $50 - $60 USD per night, while private bures start around $100 - $150 USD per night.
    - Location: Drawaqa Island, Yasawa Islands, Fiji.

Activities:

- Snorkeling: Enjoy world-class snorkeling right off the beaches of the Yasawa Islands. Bring your own snorkeling gear or rent equipment from local shops for a budget-friendly underwater adventure.

- Hiking: Lace up your hiking boots and explore the lush landscapes of the Yasawa Islands. Many islands offer hiking trails with stunning viewpoints and opportunities to encounter local wildlife.

Top Attractions in the Yasawa Islands:

- **Blue Lagoon Beach**:
  - Starting Price: Free (beach access)
  - Money Saving Tip: Pack your own snorkeling gear and spend the day exploring the vibrant coral reefs just offshore.
- **Sawa-i-Lau Caves**:
  - Starting Price: $10-20 USD (entry fee)
  - Money Saving Tip: Visit during low tide to access the caves without the need for a guided tour.
- **Nacula Island Village Visits**:
  - Starting Price: Free (visit, donations welcome)
  - Money Saving Tip: Participate in traditional village activities, such as meke performances or kava ceremonies, for an authentic cultural experience.
- **Sunset Beach** (Nacula Island):
  - Starting Price: Free (beach access)
  - Money Saving Tip: Bring your own picnic and enjoy a romantic sunset dinner on the beach.
- **Naviti Island Hiking Trails**:
  - Starting Price: Free (walk)
  - Money Saving Tip: Explore the island's hiking trails independently for stunning views of the surrounding islands.
- **Mantaray Island Marine Reserve**:
  - Starting Price: Free (snorkeling)
  - Money Saving Tip: Bring your own snorkeling gear and swim with manta rays in the marine reserve's crystal-clear waters.
- **Sunset Kayaking**:
  - Starting Price: Free (kayak rental)
  - Money Saving Tip: Rent a kayak from your accommodation and paddle out to sea for a front-row seat to the island's breathtaking sunsets.
- **Drawaqa Island Shark Snorkel**:
  - Starting Price: $30-50 USD (guided tour)
  - Money Saving Tip: Book directly through local operators for discounted rates on shark snorkeling tours.
- **Turtle Beach** (Yasawa Island):
  - Starting Price: Free (beach access)
  - Money Saving Tip: Keep an eye out for nesting turtles during the breeding season for a chance to witness this natural spectacle.
- **Octopus Resort Fire Dancing**:
  - Starting Price: Free (performance)
  - Money Saving Tip: Enjoy complimentary fire dancing performances at Octopus Resort while sipping on a cocktail from the bar.
- **Sawa-i-Lau Lagoon**:
  - Starting Price: Free (swimming)
  - Money Saving Tip: Swim in the turquoise waters of Sawa-i-Lau Lagoon, known for its stunning underwater caves and rock formations.
- **Nanuya Lailai Island**:
  - Starting Price: Free (beach access)

- Money Saving Tip: Spend the day exploring the pristine beaches and hiking trails of Nanuya Lailai Island without spending a dime.
- **Fiji Beach Volleyball Tournament**:
  - Starting Price: Free (spectator)
  - Money Saving Tip: Watch local beach volleyball tournaments for free entertainment and a glimpse into Fijian sports culture.
- **Naviti Island Snorkeling**:
  - Starting Price: Free (snorkeling)
  - Money Saving Tip: Bring your own snorkeling gear and explore the vibrant coral reefs surrounding Naviti Island.
- **Wayalailai Ecohaven Waterfall Hike**:
  - Starting Price: $10-20 USD (guided hike)
  - Money Saving Tip: Join a group hike to Wayalailai Ecohaven Waterfall for discounted rates and the opportunity to meet fellow travelers.
- **Sunset Beach Yoga**:
  - Starting Price: Free (group session)
  - Money Saving Tip: Join a complimentary beach yoga session offered by your accommodation for a relaxing end to the day.
- **Sawailau Island Snorkeling**:
  - Starting Price: Free (snorkeling)
  - Money Saving Tip: Explore the underwater caves and marine life surrounding Sawailau Island with your own snorkeling gear.
- **Kuata Island Village Tour**:
  - Starting Price: Free (visit, donations welcome)
  - Money Saving Tip: Learn about traditional Fijian customs and daily life during a guided village tour on Kuata Island.
- **Nanuya Balavu Island Beach Picnic**:
  - Starting Price: Free (beach access)
  - Money Saving Tip: Pack a picnic lunch and spend the day lounging on the pristine beaches of Nanuya Balavu Island.
- **Manta Ray Snorkeling**:
  - Starting Price: $30-50 USD (guided tour)
  - Money Saving Tip: Book manta ray snorkeling tours during the off-peak season for lower prices and fewer crowds.

Fiji’s Marine Life

Exploring the marine life in Fiji, especially around Yasawa is an adventure filled with vibrant coral reefs, diverse fish species, and fascinating underwater ecosystems. Here's an in-depth guide to the marine life you can encounter in Fiji:

- **Coral Reefs**:
  - Fiji is renowned for its extensive coral reefs, which are home to a dazzling array of marine organisms. Hard corals, such as staghorn and brain corals, dominate the reef structures, providing essential habitat for a myriad of species. Soft corals, including sea fans and whip corals, add bursts of color and texture to the underwater landscape.
- **Fish Species**:
  - Fiji's waters teem with an astonishing diversity of fish species, ranging from tiny reef fish to large pelagics. Common reef inhabitants include vibrant parrotfish, graceful butterflyfish, and colorful anthias. Look out for larger species like barracudas, groupers, and trevallies patrolling the reef edges. You may also encounter reef sharks, such as white-tip and black-tip reef sharks, cruising along the reef slopes.
- **Invertebrates**:
  - Fiji's reefs are home to a fascinating array of invertebrates, including crustaceans, mollusks, and echinoderms. Keep an eye out for intricate nudibranchs, colorful sea stars, and elusive octopuses camouflaged among the coral crevices. Crustaceans like hermit crabs and colorful shrimp add to the vibrant tapestry of marine life.
- **Cephalopods**:
  - Fiji's waters are inhabited by various cephalopods, including octopuses, squids, and cuttlefish. These intelligent creatures display remarkable camouflage abilities and are often encountered during night dives or twilight reef explorations. Watch as octopuses change color and texture to blend seamlessly with their surroundings, or marvel at the mesmerizing displays of cuttlefish as they communicate through color patterns.
- **Marine Mammals**:
  - While exploring Fiji's waters, you may have the opportunity to encounter marine mammals such as dolphins and whales. Several species of dolphins, including spinner dolphins and bottlenose dolphins, frequent Fiji's coastal waters, delighting snorkelers and divers with their playful antics. During the winter months (July to September), humpback whales migrate through Fiji's waters, providing unforgettable opportunities for whale watching and listening to their haunting songs.

Waya Island

Tucked away in the heart of Fiji's Yasawa archipelago, Waya Island emerges as a pristine paradise, captivating travelers with its rugged landscapes, secluded beaches, and vibrant coral reefs. As one of the jewels of the Yasawa Islands, Waya exudes an irresistible charm, offering visitors a sanctuary of relaxation, adventure, and cultural immersion. Join us as we embark on a journey to uncover the enchanting allure of this idyllic gem.

Waya Island, surrounded by the crystal-clear waters of the South Pacific, is renowned for its breathtaking natural beauty and serene ambiance. The island's dramatic cliffs rise majestically from the sea, giving way to verdant hillsides carpeted with lush tropical vegetation. Fringed by powdery white sands and swaying coconut palms, Waya's beaches provide the perfect setting for sunbathing, swimming, and water sports, making it a haven for beach lovers and outdoor enthusiasts alike.

One of the most captivating features of Waya Island is its vibrant coral reefs, which teem with a kaleidoscope of marine life. The surrounding waters are home to colorful fish, graceful sea turtles, and majestic manta rays, inviting snorkelers and divers to explore their underwater wonders. Dive into the crystal-clear lagoon and discover hidden caves, coral gardens, and underwater pinnacles that abound with life and beauty.

But Waya Island is not just a paradise for water lovers—it's also a playground for adventure seekers and nature enthusiasts. Embark on hiking trails that wind through the island's lush interior, offering panoramic views of the surrounding ocean and neighboring islands. Explore hidden waterfalls, natural swimming holes, and ancient archaeological sites nestled amidst the island's rugged terrain, where you can immerse yourself in the natural wonders of Fiji.

For those seeking a taste of Fijian culture and tradition, Waya Island offers opportunities to connect with the local community and learn about the island's rich heritage. Visit traditional Fijian villages where you can participate in kava ceremonies, witness traditional dances, and learn about age-old customs and traditions passed down through generations. Sample delicious Fijian cuisine at one of the island's local eateries, where fresh seafood, tropical fruits, and indigenous spices combine to create a culinary experience like no other.

Affordable Accommodation Options:

While Waya Island offers luxury resorts, there are budget-friendly accommodations suitable for the thrifty traveler:

- **Octopus Resort - Dormitory Beds**:
- Octopus Resort offers budget-friendly dormitory beds ideal for solo travelers or budget-conscious groups.
- Prices: Dormitory beds start at around $30 - $40 USD per night, including meals.
- Enjoy access to the resort's amenities and activities, including snorkeling, kayaking, and cultural performances.

Korovou Island

Nestled within the picturesque Yasawa archipelago of Fiji, Korovou Island emerges as a hidden gem, enchanting travelers with its pristine beaches, turquoise waters, and laid-back island vibe. As one of the captivating destinations within the Yasawa Islands, Korovou offers visitors a serene sanctuary where they can unwind, explore, and immerse themselves in the natural beauty and cultural richness of Fiji. Join us as we embark on a journey to discover the captivating allure of Korovou Island.

Korovou Island, surrounded by the crystal-clear waters of the South Pacific, boasts a landscape characterized by soft sandy shores, swaying coconut palms, and lush tropical vegetation. The island's idyllic beaches provide the perfect backdrop for relaxation, whether you're lounging under the shade of a palm tree, strolling along the shoreline, or indulging in water sports such as snorkeling and kayaking in the tranquil lagoon. With its serene ambiance and pristine surroundings, Korovou invites visitors to embrace the slow pace of island life and savor every moment of their stay.

One of the highlights of Korovou Island is its vibrant underwater world, teeming with marine life and coral reefs. Snorkelers and divers will delight in exploring the kaleidoscope of colors beneath the surface, where they can encounter tropical fish, vibrant corals, and other fascinating creatures. Dive into the warm waters and discover hidden caves, underwater gardens, and mesmerizing marine landscapes, or simply float atop the gentle waves and marvel at the beauty that surrounds you.

But Korovou Island is not just a paradise for water enthusiasts—it also offers opportunities for land-based adventures and cultural experiences. Embark on guided hikes through the island's lush interior, where you can discover hidden waterfalls, ancient ruins, and panoramic viewpoints that offer sweeping vistas of the surrounding ocean. Visit nearby Fijian villages and immerse yourself in the local culture, participating in traditional ceremonies, learning about traditional crafts, and sampling delicious Fijian cuisine prepared with fresh, locally sourced ingredients.

Affordable Accommodation Options:

While Korovou Island offers luxury resorts, there are budget-friendly accommodations suitable for the thrifty traveler:

- **Barefoot Kuata Island - Dormitory Beds**:
- Barefoot Kuata Island offers budget-friendly dormitory beds ideal for solo travelers or budget-conscious groups.
- Prices: Dormitory beds start at around $30 - $40 USD per night, including meals.
- Enjoy access to the resort's amenities and activities, including snorkeling, kayaking, and cultural performances.

Nacula Island

Nacula Island, located in the northern reaches of the Yasawa archipelago, is renowned for its stunning natural landscapes and secluded beaches. The island is characterized by rugged terrain, with verdant hillsides cascading down to powdery white sands and crystal-clear waters. Fringed by vibrant coral reefs, Nacula offers unparalleled opportunities for snorkeling, diving, and water sports, making it a haven for outdoor enthusiasts and marine adventurers alike.

Affordable Accommodation Options:

While Nacula Island offers luxury resorts, there are budget-friendly accommodations suitable for the thrifty traveler:

- **Gold Coast Resort**:
- Gold Coast Resort offers budget-friendly accommodation options including dormitory beds and traditional bures (bungalows).
- Prices: Dormitory beds start at around $30 - $40 USD per night, while basic bures start at around $80 - $100 USD per night.

Taveuni

Taveuni, whose name means "Water in the Land" in Fijian, is the third-largest island in Fiji and is renowned for its breathtaking landscapes and pristine ecosystems. The island is a haven for nature lovers and outdoor enthusiasts, boasting an incredible array of flora and fauna found nowhere else on Earth. From rare orchids and exotic birds to endemic species of plants and animals, Taveuni is a treasure trove of biodiversity waiting to be explored.

One of the most iconic features of Taveuni is its network of lush rainforests, which cover much of the island's interior. Protected within the boundaries of Bouma National Heritage Park, these ancient forests are home to towering hardwood trees, winding rivers, and hidden waterfalls that cascade down verdant slopes. Hiking trails crisscross the park, leading to stunning viewpoints, secluded swimming holes, and breathtaking vistas of the surrounding landscape.

But Taveuni's natural beauty extends beyond its rainforests to its pristine coastline, where crystal-clear waters and vibrant coral reefs await exploration. The island is surrounded by a marine reserve teeming with marine life, making it a paradise for snorkelers, divers, and underwater enthusiasts. Swim alongside colorful fish, sea turtles, and reef sharks in waters of unparalleled clarity, or explore underwater caves and coral gardens in search of hidden treasures.

For those seeking a taste of adventure and adrenaline, Taveuni offers a range of outdoor activities and eco-tours to suit every interest and skill level. Trek to the summit of Des Voeux Peak, the highest point on the island, for panoramic views of the surrounding islands and distant horizons. Kayak along the island's rugged coastline, exploring hidden coves, secluded beaches, and secret lagoons hidden from the beaten path.

But Taveuni is not just a playground for outdoor enthusiasts—it's also a sanctuary for relaxation and rejuvenation. Luxury resorts and eco-lodges dot the island's shores, offering a range of amenities and activities designed to pamper and indulge. From beachfront villas with private plunge pools to overwater bungalows with uninterrupted ocean views, accommodations in Taveuni are the epitome of tropical luxury.

And no visit to Taveuni would be complete without experiencing its vibrant culture and traditions. Visit traditional Fijian villages nestled in the highlands, where you can participate in kava ceremonies, witness traditional dances, and learn about age-old customs passed down through generations. Sample delicious Fijian cuisine at one of the island's gourmet restaurants, where fresh seafood, tropical fruits, and exotic spices combine to create an unforgettable dining experience.

Getting to Taveuni on a Budget:

The most cost-effective way to reach Taveuni is by taking advantage of Fiji's domestic flight options:

- **Domestic Flight from Nadi or Suva**:
- Fiji Airways and Northern Air offer daily flights from Nadi International Airport or Suva's Nausori International Airport to Matei Airport on Taveuni.
- Prices: One-way flights start at around $100 - $150 USD per person, depending on the season and availability.
- Book in advance and consider flying during off-peak times for the best deals.

Affordable Accommodation Options:

While Taveuni is known for its luxury resorts, there are budget-friendly accommodations available for the savvy traveler:

- **Garden Island Resort**:
  - Located in Waiyevo, Garden Island Resort offers budget-friendly rooms with garden views.
  - Prices: Starting at around $80 - $100 USD per night for a standard room.
  - Amenities include a swimming pool, restaurant, and easy access to local attractions.
- **Taveuni Dive Resort**:
  - This eco-friendly resort offers budget-friendly accommodations with options for dormitory beds and private rooms.

    - Prices: Dormitory beds start at around $30 - $40 USD per night, while private rooms start at around $70 - $80 USD per night.
    - Perfect for budget-conscious travelers interested in diving and exploring the island's marine life.

Budget-Friendly Eats:

Sampling local cuisine doesn't have to break the bank. Here are some affordable dining options on Taveuni:

- **Local Markets and Food Stalls**:
    - Visit the local markets in Waiyevo or Matei for budget-friendly meals like curry dishes, grilled seafood, and fresh tropical fruits.
    - Prices: Meals can range from $5 - $10 USD per person, depending on your choices.
- **Taveuni Eats**:
    - This casual eatery offers a variety of Fijian and international dishes at affordable prices.
    - Prices: Main dishes start at around $8 - $15 USD per person, with vegetarian options available.

Free Attractions and Activities:

Discover the natural beauty of Taveuni without spending a dime with these free attractions:

- **Tavoro Waterfalls**:
    - Explore the lush jungle trails of Bouma National Heritage Park and discover the three tiers of Tavoro Waterfalls.
    - Admission: Free, but donations are welcome.
- **Lavena Coastal Walk**:
    - Embark on a scenic coastal walk along the rugged coastline of Taveuni, passing through lush forests and pristine beaches.
    - Admission: Free, though guided tours may have a small fee.
- **Snorkeling at Waitabu Marine Park**:
    - Bring your snorkeling gear and explore the vibrant coral reefs and marine life at Waitabu Marine Park.
    - Admission: Free, though donations are appreciated for conservation efforts.
- **Village Visits**:
    - Immerse yourself in Fijian culture with a visit to one of Taveuni's traditional villages. Engage with locals, learn about their customs, and experience authentic island hospitality.
    - Admission: Free, but it's customary to bring a small gift or make a donation to the village.

Beqa Island

Beqa Island, named after the legendary Fijian war canoe, is located just off the southern coast of Viti Levu, Fiji's main island. Despite its proximity to the bustling mainland, Beqa remains a pristine and untouched oasis, with lush rainforests, cascading waterfalls, and secluded beaches waiting to be discovered. The island is surrounded by a protected marine sanctuary, home to some of the most spectacular coral reefs and marine life in the South Pacific.

One of the most iconic features of Beqa Island is its vibrant coral reefs, which teem with a kaleidoscope of marine life. The island is renowned for its world-class diving and snorkeling opportunities, with dive sites such as the famous Beqa Lagoon offering encounters with reef sharks, manta rays, and colorful tropical fish. Dive into the crystal-clear waters and explore underwater caves, coral gardens, and ancient shipwrecks in search of hidden treasures.

But Beqa Island is not just for underwater enthusiasts—it's also a paradise for outdoor adventurers and nature lovers alike. Hike through the island's lush rainforests, where winding trails lead to hidden waterfalls, natural swimming pools, and panoramic viewpoints offering sweeping vistas of the surrounding landscapes. Explore traditional Fijian villages nestled in the highlands, where you can participate in kava ceremonies, witness traditional dances, and learn about age-old customs passed down through generations.

For those seeking a taste of luxury and indulgence, Beqa Island offers a range of upscale resorts and eco-lodges, each offering a unique blend of comfort and sophistication. From beachfront villas with private plunge pools to overwater bungalows with uninterrupted ocean views, accommodations on Beqa Island are designed to pamper and delight, providing the perfect retreat for honeymooners, couples, and families alike.

And no visit to Beqa Island would be complete without experiencing a traditional Fijian firewalking ceremony, where brave warriors walk barefoot across hot coals in a display of strength, courage, and cultural tradition. Join the local community in celebrating this ancient ritual, which has been practiced on the island for centuries, and immerse yourself in the warmth and hospitality of the Fijian people.

Getting to Beqa Island on a Budget:

Beqa Island is accessible via boat or ferry from Viti Levu. Here's the most cost-effective way to reach Beqa Island:

- **Ferry from Pacific Harbour**:
- Beqa Island is just a short boat ride away from Pacific Harbour on the mainland.
- Prices: Ferry tickets typically cost around $20 - $30 USD per person for a one-way trip.
- Book your ferry tickets in advance to ensure availability, especially during peak seasons.

Affordable Accommodation Options:

While Beqa Island is known for its luxury resorts, there are budget-friendly accommodations available for the budget-conscious traveler:

- **Beqa Lagoon Resort**:
- Beqa Lagoon Resort offers budget-friendly accommodation options including dormitory beds and basic bures (bungalows).
- Prices: Dormitory beds start at around $40 - $50 USD per night, while basic bures start at around $80 - $100 USD per night.
- Enjoy access to the resort's amenities and activities, including snorkeling and kayaking.

Kadavu Island

Kadavu Island, the fourth-largest island in Fiji, is located to the south of the main island of Viti Levu. Despite its size, Kadavu remains relatively untouched by tourism, retaining its natural beauty and authentic Fijian charm. The island is characterized by rugged terrain, with verdant rainforests covering much of its interior and fringing coral reefs surrounding its coastline.

One of the most striking features of Kadavu Island is its vibrant underwater world, which teems with a kaleidoscope of marine life. The Great Astrolabe Reef, one of the largest barrier reefs in the world, encircles much of the island, offering unparalleled diving and snorkeling opportunities. Swim alongside colorful fish, graceful manta rays, and majestic reef sharks as you explore the reef's pristine coral gardens and underwater caves.

But Kadavu Island is not just for underwater enthusiasts—it's also a paradise for outdoor adventurers and nature lovers alike. Hike through the island's lush rainforests, where winding trails lead to hidden waterfalls, natural swimming pools, and panoramic viewpoints offering sweeping vistas of the surrounding landscapes. Birdwatchers will delight in the chance to spot endemic species such as the Kadavu musk parrot and the Kadavu honeyeater in their natural habitat.

For those seeking a taste of Fijian culture and tradition, Kadavu Island offers opportunities to connect with the local community and learn about the island's rich heritage. Visit traditional Fijian villages nestled along the coast, where you can participate in kava ceremonies, witness traditional dances, and learn about age-old customs passed down through generations. Sample delicious Fijian cuisine at one of the island's local eateries, where fresh seafood, tropical fruits, and exotic spices combine to create an unforgettable dining experience.

And no visit to Kadavu Island would be complete without experiencing its warm hospitality and laid-back atmosphere. Stay in a traditional Fijian bure, or bungalow, where you can fall asleep to the sound of the waves lapping against the shore and wake up to breathtaking views of the sunrise over the ocean. Immerse yourself in the rhythm of island life as you relax on the beach, paddle through tranquil lagoons, or simply unwind with a book under the shade of a palm tree.

Getting to Kadavu Island on a Budget:

Kadavu Island is accessible by boat or plane from Viti Levu, Fiji's main island. Here's the most cost-effective way to reach Kadavu Island:

- **Ferry from Suva or Viti Levu**:
  - Kadavu Island can be reached by ferry from Suva or other ports on Viti Levu.
  - Prices: Ferry tickets typically cost around $50 - $70 USD per person for a one-way trip, depending on the departure point and the ferry company.
  - Book your ferry tickets in advance, especially during peak travel seasons, to secure your spot.
- **Domestic Flight**:
  - Fiji Airways and other domestic airlines operate flights from Nadi International Airport or Suva's Nausori International Airport to Kadavu Island.
  - Prices: One-way flights start at around $100 - $150 USD per person, depending on the season and availability.
  - Look for promotional deals and book your flights in advance for the best prices.

Affordable Accommodation Options:

While Kadavu Island offers luxury resorts, there are budget-friendly accommodations suitable for the frugal traveler:

- **Kadavu Koro Eco Resort**:

- Kadavu Koro Eco Resort offers budget-friendly accommodation options including dormitory beds and traditional bures (bungalows).
- Prices: Dormitory beds start at around $30 - $40 USD per night, while basic bures start at around $80 - $100 USD per night.
- Enjoy access to the resort's amenities and activities, including snorkeling, kayaking, and hiking.

Sampling local cuisine is a must while visiting Kadavu Island. Here are some affordable dining options to consider:

- Explore the villages on Kadavu Island and discover local eateries and food stalls serving authentic Fijian dishes.
- Prices: Meals can range from $5 - $10 USD per person, depending on your choices.

Free Attractions and Activities:

Discover the natural beauty and cultural heritage of Kadavu Island without spending a dime with these free attractions and activities:

- **Beachcombing and Swimming**:
  - Spend your days exploring Kadavu Island's pristine beaches, collecting seashells, and swimming in the crystal-clear waters of the Pacific Ocean.
  - Admission: Free.
- **Hiking and Nature Walks**:
  - Embark on self-guided hikes through Kadavu Island's lush rainforests, where you can discover hidden waterfalls, exotic flora, and native wildlife.
  - Admission: Free.

Qamea Island

Qamea Island, located in the remote northern reaches of Fiji, boasts a landscape characterized by rugged cliffs, verdant rainforests, and powdery white sands lapped by crystal-clear waters. Fringed by vibrant coral reefs teeming with marine life, Qamea offers unparalleled opportunities for snorkeling, diving, and water sports, making it a paradise for outdoor enthusiasts and nature lovers alike.

One of the most captivating features of Qamea Island is its pristine beaches, which provide the perfect setting for relaxation and rejuvenation. Whether you're lounging in a hammock beneath the shade of a palm tree, soaking up the sun on the soft sands, or swimming in the warm, turquoise waters, Qamea's beaches offer blissful moments of tranquility and serenity.

But Qamea Island is not just a haven for beach lovers—it's also a playground for adventure seekers and cultural explorers. Embark on hiking trails that wind through the island's lush interior, where you can discover hidden waterfalls, natural swimming holes, and panoramic viewpoints offering breathtaking vistas of the surrounding ocean and neighboring islands. Explore nearby uninhabited islets on a kayak or paddleboard, or join a guided tour to explore the island's hidden treasures and secret spots.

For those seeking a taste of Fijian culture and tradition, Qamea Island offers opportunities to connect with the local community and learn about the island's rich heritage. Visit traditional Fijian villages where you can participate in kava ceremonies, witness traditional dances, and learn about age-old customs and traditions passed down through generations. Sample delicious Fijian cuisine at one of the island's restaurants, where fresh seafood, tropical fruits, and indigenous spices combine to create a culinary experience like no other.

And no visit to Qamea Island would be complete without experiencing its warm hospitality and laid-back atmosphere. Stay in a traditional Fijian bure, or bungalow, where you can fall asleep to the sound of the waves lapping against the shore and wake up to breathtaking views of the sunrise over the ocean. Immerse yourself in the rhythm of island life as you relax on the beach, explore the island's natural wonders, and forge lasting memories with loved ones.

- **Domestic Flight from Nadi or Suva**:
- Fiji Airways and Northern Air offer daily flights from Nadi International Airport or Suva's Nausori International Airport to Taveuni Airport.
- From Taveuni, you can take a short boat transfer to Qamea Island.
- Prices: One-way flights start at around $100 - $150 USD per person to Taveuni, with additional costs for the boat transfer to Qamea Island.
- Book in advance and consider flying during off-peak times for the best deals.

While Qamea Island offers luxury resorts, there are budget-friendly accommodations suitable for the thrifty traveler:

- **Qamea Resort and Spa - Garden Bure**:
- Qamea Resort and Spa offers Garden Bure accommodation options ideal for budget-conscious travelers.
- Prices: Garden Bures start at around $150 - $200 USD per night, depending on the season and availability.
- Enjoy access to the resort's amenities and activities, including snorkeling, kayaking, and cultural experiences.

Savusavu

Savusavu, nestled on the southeastern coast of Vanua Levu, Fiji's second-largest island, is a charming waterfront town renowned for its natural beauty, warm hospitality, and rich cultural heritage. Known as the "Hidden Paradise of Fiji," Savusavu exudes a relaxed atmosphere and offers visitors a unique blend of tropical adventure, rejuvenation, and authentic Fijian experiences. Join us as we explore the enchanting allure of Savusavu and uncover its many treasures.

Surrounded by lush rainforests, verdant hillsides, and pristine coastlines, Savusavu captivates travelers with its stunning natural landscapes and tranquil ambiance. The town's picturesque waterfront is lined with palm-fringed beaches, offering panoramic views of the azure Koro Sea and the verdant hills beyond. With its crystal-clear waters and vibrant coral reefs, Savusavu is a paradise for snorkelers, divers, and water sports enthusiasts, who can explore the underwater wonders of Namena Marine Reserve, one of Fiji's most biodiverse marine sanctuaries.

But Savusavu is not just a destination for marine adventures—it also boasts a rich cultural heritage and a vibrant local community. Explore the town's bustling markets, where you can sample fresh tropical fruits, handcrafted souvenirs, and delicious Fijian cuisine prepared with locally sourced ingredients. Visit traditional Fijian villages nestled in the surrounding hills, where you can participate in kava ceremonies, learn about traditional crafts such as weaving and pottery, and immerse yourself in the warmth and hospitality of the local people.

For those seeking relaxation and rejuvenation, Savusavu offers a range of wellness experiences and luxury resorts nestled amidst its pristine landscapes. Indulge in a pampering spa treatment overlooking the ocean, practice yoga on the beach at sunrise, or simply unwind in a hammock beneath the swaying palms. With its serene ambiance and natural beauty, Savusavu provides the perfect setting for wellness retreats, romantic getaways, and unforgettable vacations.

Venture beyond the town limits and discover the natural wonders of Savusavu's hinterland, where lush rainforests, cascading waterfalls, and hidden hot springs await exploration. Embark on guided hikes through the verdant wilderness of Waisali Rainforest Reserve, where you can encounter rare native birds, towering hardwood trees, and breathtaking vistas of the surrounding landscape. Take a dip in the warm waters of Savusavu's natural hot springs, renowned for their therapeutic properties and rejuvenating effects on mind, body, and soul.

Getting to Savusavu on a Budget:

Savusavu is accessible by plane or ferry from Viti Levu. Here's the most cost-effective way to reach Savusavu:

- **Domestic Flight from Nadi or Suva**:
- Fiji Airways and Northern Air offer daily flights from Nadi International Airport or Suva's Nausori International Airport to Savusavu Airport.
- Prices: One-way flights start at around $100 - $150 USD per person, depending on the season and availability.

Understanding Fiji's flora and fauna

The most enchanting treasures come with no price tag at all!

Flora of Fiji:

Fiji's plant life is as diverse as it is enchanting.

1. Tropical Rainforests:

Step into the heart of Fiji's tropical rainforests, and you'll be greeted by a lush green canopy that teems with life. Here, towering trees such as the native Dakua or Vesi provide shelter to a myriad of plant species, from ferns and mosses to towering tree ferns. Keep an eye out for the vibrant blooms of the Fijian ginger (Dale's Wilder), whose fiery red flowers add a splash of color to the forest floor.

2. Coastal Mangroves:

Venture to Fiji's coastal regions, and you'll discover the intricate ecosystems of mangrove forests, where salt-tolerant trees and shrubs thrive in brackish waters. Keep an eye out for the distinctive prop roots of the mangrove trees, which provide vital habitat for fish, crabs, and other marine creatures. Look for the delicate mangrove ferns and orchids that cling to the branches, adding a touch of beauty to these coastal sanctuaries.

3. Coral Reefs:

Beneath the shimmering waters that surround Fiji's islands lies a kaleidoscope of coral reefs, home to an astonishing diversity of marine life. While snorkeling or diving, keep an eye out for the colorful corals that form the backbone of these ecosystems, from branching staghorn corals to massive brain corals. Look for vibrant reef fish darting among the corals, including parrotfish, butterflyfish, and clownfish, each adding their own splash of color to the underwater landscape.

Fauna of Fiji:

Now, let's turn our attention to the fascinating fauna that calls Fiji home, from the iconic birds that soar through the skies to the elusive creatures that roam the forests and seas.

1. Birdlife:

Fiji is a paradise for birdwatchers, with over 100 species of birds inhabiting its forests, wetlands, and coastal areas. Look to the skies, and you may spot the vibrant plumage of the Fiji parrotfinch, the majestic flight of the collared lory, or the distinctive call of the orange dove. Keep an eye out for the elusive silktail, a rare bird found only in Fiji's montane forests, with its long, flowing tail and melodious song.

2. Marine Life:

Dive beneath the waves, and you'll discover a dazzling array of marine life that inhabits Fiji's coral reefs and seagrass beds. Keep an eye out for graceful manta rays gliding through the water, sea turtles lazily grazing on seagrass, and reef sharks patrolling the depths. Look for colorful nudibranchs and sea slugs hiding among the corals, as well as elusive creatures such as the blue ribbon eel and the flamboyant cuttlefish.

3. Land Mammals:

While Fiji may not be known for its terrestrial mammals, the islands are home to a variety of creatures, including bats, rodents, and introduced species such as pigs and deer. Keep an eye out for the Fiji flying fox, a large fruit bat with a wingspan of over a meter, which plays a vital role in pollinating native plants and dispersing seeds. Look for the endemic Fiji ground frog, a small terrestrial frog found in the forests and grasslands of the islands, known for its distinctive chirping call.

Conservation Efforts:

As you explore Fiji's natural wonders, it's important to remember the importance of conservation efforts in preserving these fragile ecosystems. From marine protected areas to reforestation projects, organizations and local communities are working together to safeguard Fiji's biodiversity for future generations to enjoy.

Exploring the unique flora and fauna of Fiji doesn't have to break the bank! Here are some of the best spots to experience Fiji's natural wonders for free:

- **Koroyanitu National Heritage Park (Viti Levu):** This protected area encompasses rugged mountains, lush rainforests, and cascading waterfalls, offering excellent opportunities to explore Fiji's diverse flora and fauna. Take a hike along the park's trails to encounter native plant species, colorful birds, and stunning viewpoints overlooking the surrounding landscape.
- **Colo-i-Suva Forest Park (Viti Levu):** Located just outside Suva, Colo-i-Suva Forest Park is a tranquil oasis of lush vegetation, pristine streams, and tropical birdlife. Wander along the park's walking trails to discover ancient mahogany trees, fern-lined gullies, and hidden swimming holes, all while keeping an eye out for colorful birds such as the Fiji parrotfinch and the collared lory.
- **Tavoro Waterfalls (Taveuni):** Situated within Bouma National Heritage Park on the island of Taveuni, the Tavoro Waterfalls are a series of three stunning waterfalls surrounded by lush rainforest. Take a hike through the park's verdant trails to reach these cascading falls, where you can cool off in the refreshing pools and admire the diverse plant life that thrives in this pristine environment.

- **Lavena Coastal Walk (Taveuni):** This scenic coastal trail winds its way along the rugged coastline of Taveuni, offering panoramic views of the ocean and opportunities to encounter Fiji's unique flora and fauna. Keep an eye out for colorful birds, exotic flowers, and towering banyan trees as you explore this picturesque stretch of coastline.
- **Sabeto Valley (Viti Levu):** Nestled between the Sabeto Mountains, the Sabeto Valley is a fertile agricultural region known for its lush vegetation and traditional villages. Take a leisurely stroll through the valley to admire the vibrant tropical gardens, fruit orchards, and swaying coconut palms, all while soaking in the tranquil beauty of the surrounding landscape.
- **Sigatoka Sand Dunes National Park (Viti Levu):** This protected area on the Coral Coast of Viti Levu is home to Fiji's largest sand dunes, as well as a variety of unique plant species adapted to the harsh coastal environment. Explore the park's walking trails to discover native coastal vegetation, including salt-tolerant shrubs, grasses, and wildflowers, as well as the occasional glimpse of native birds and reptiles.
- **Nausori Highlands (Viti Levu):** Located in the interior of Viti Levu, the Nausori Highlands offer sweeping views of the surrounding mountains, valleys, and rivers, as well as opportunities to encounter Fiji's native flora and fauna. Take a scenic drive through the highlands or embark on a hiking adventure to discover hidden waterfalls, lush forests, and tranquil streams, all while immersing yourself in the natural beauty of Fiji's interior.

Night Time Freebies

While Fiji is renowned for its stunning beaches and adventurous daytime activities, the fun doesn't end when the sun sets. There are plenty of free and enjoyable nighttime activities to indulge in without spending a penny. So, slip into your flip-flops, grab your sense of adventure, and let's explore what Fiji has to offer after dark!

1. Stargazing on the Beach:

Fiji's clear night skies provide the perfect backdrop for a mesmerizing stargazing experience. Head to the nearest beach away from city lights, lay out a blanket, and gaze up at the twinkling stars above. With the soothing sound of waves lapping against the shore as your soundtrack, you'll feel like you're floating among the constellations.

2. Cultural Performances:

Many resorts and villages in Fiji host traditional cultural performances in the evenings, showcasing the vibrant dances, music, and storytelling of the local Fijian culture. These performances often take place around a bonfire under the stars, creating a magical atmosphere that transports you back in time. Check with your accommodation or nearby villages to see if any cultural performances are scheduled during your stay.

3. Beach Bonfires and Drum Circles:

Gather around a crackling bonfire on the beach and join in a lively drum circle with fellow travelers and locals. Feel the rhythm pulsating through your veins as you dance barefoot in the sand beneath the moonlit sky. It's a communal experience that fosters connections and creates lasting memories, all while enjoying the beauty of Fiji's natural surroundings.

4. Nighttime Wildlife Encounters:

Take a moonlit stroll through Fiji's lush landscapes and keep an eye out for nocturnal wildlife that comes alive after dark. Listen for the calls of native birds, spot geckos clinging to tree branches, or search for bioluminescent creatures in the water. Nature's nighttime symphony offers a captivating glimpse into Fiji's diverse ecosystem.

5. Fire Dancing Performances:

Many resorts and beachfront bars in Fiji host fire dancing performances in the evenings, where skilled performers twirl and spin fiery batons to the beat of traditional Fijian music. Watch in awe as the flames dance against the backdrop of the night sky, creating a mesmerizing display of light and motion.

6. Night Markets and Festivals:

If you're visiting Fiji during a local festival or special event, be sure to check out the vibrant night markets that come to life after dark. Browse stalls selling handmade crafts, sample delicious street food, and immerse yourself in the lively atmosphere of Fijian culture.

7. Beachfront Movie Nights:

Some resorts and beach bars in Fiji host outdoor movie nights on the beach, where guests can gather under the stars to watch classic films or blockbuster hits. Snuggle up with a cozy blanket and a bucket of popcorn as you enjoy a movie night with a view.

With these free nighttime activities, you can continue your adventure in Fiji long after the sun dips below the horizon. So, embrace the magic of the night and create unforgettable memories under Fiji's starlit skies.

Getting Out Cheaply

1. **Flights:**

- **Budget Airlines:** Look for budget airlines operating in the region, such as Fiji Airways' subsidiary, Fiji Link, or other low-cost carriers like Jetstar Airways or Air New Zealand's subsidiary, Air Nelson. These airlines often offer competitive fares, especially if you book well in advance.
- **Flexible Dates:** Be flexible with your travel dates to take advantage of lower fares. Mid-week flights tend to be cheaper than those on weekends, and traveling during the off-peak season can also result in significant savings.
- **Use Flight Comparison Sites:** Utilize flight comparison websites like Skyscanner, Google Flights, or Kayak to compare prices across different airlines and booking platforms. Set up price alerts to notify you when fares drop for your desired route.
- **Redeem Travel Rewards:** If you have accumulated frequent flyer miles or travel rewards points, consider using them to offset the cost of your flight. Many airlines offer reward seats or discounted fares for loyal customers.

2. **Ferries:**

- **Inter-Island Ferries:** If you're traveling between the main islands of Fiji, such as Viti Levu and Vanua Levu, consider taking an inter-island ferry. Companies like Patterson Brothers Shipping and Goundar Shipping offer regular ferry services at affordable rates.
- **Advance Booking:** Book your ferry tickets in advance to secure the best fares and guarantee your seat, especially during peak travel periods or on popular routes.
- **Consider Overnight Ferries:** Overnight ferry services are available between certain islands, allowing you to save on accommodation costs for a night while also enjoying a unique travel experience.

3. **Bus and Land Transport:**

- **Public Buses:** Utilize Fiji's public bus network for budget-friendly land transport between towns and cities. Buses are generally inexpensive and provide a convenient way to explore the islands.
- **Shared Taxis and Rideshares:** Consider sharing a taxi or using ridesharing services like Uber or Ola to split the cost of transportation with other travelers. Negotiate fares in advance to ensure you're getting a fair price.
- **Renting a Bicycle:** In some areas, renting a bicycle can be a cost-effective way to get around, allowing you to explore at your own pace while saving money on transportation.

4. **Cheap Onward Destinations:**

- **Southeast Asia:** Consider traveling to neighboring Southeast Asian countries like Thailand, Indonesia, or Malaysia, where you can find budget-friendly accommodations, delicious street food, and stunning natural attractions.
- **South Pacific Islands:** Explore other South Pacific destinations like Samoa, Tonga, or Vanuatu, which offer similar tropical experiences to Fiji at a fraction of the cost.

- **New Zealand:** If you're looking for adventure, consider hopping over to New Zealand, where you can explore breathtaking landscapes, hike scenic trails, and indulge in adrenaline-pumping activities like bungee jumping or skydiving.

- **Search Comparison Websites:** Utilize flight comparison websites like Skyscanner, Kayak, or Google Flights to compare prices from different airlines and booking platforms. These platforms often offer filters to help you find the cheapest options for onward flights from Fiji to your desired destination.
- **Be Flexible with Dates:** Flexibility with your travel dates can lead to significant savings. Use the flexible date search option on flight comparison websites to see which days offer the lowest fares for your onward journey.
- **Consider Budget Airlines:** Look for budget airlines that operate routes from Fiji to your desired destination. Airlines like Jetstar Airways, Fiji Link, and Air New Zealand often offer competitive prices for flights within the South Pacific region.
- **Book in Advance:** Booking your onward flight well in advance can help you secure lower fares. Keep an eye out for special promotions and sales offered by airlines, especially during off-peak travel seasons.
- **Opt for Connecting Flights:** Consider booking connecting flights instead of direct flights, as they can sometimes be cheaper. However, be mindful of layover times and potential additional costs associated with longer travel durations.

Cheapest Airport Lounges in Fiji:

- **Fiji Airways Premier Lounge (Nadi International Airport):** Fiji Airways operates its own Premier Lounge at Nadi International Airport. While it may not be the cheapest option, it offers amenities such as comfortable seating, complimentary snacks and beverages, Wi-Fi, and shower facilities. Prices for access vary depending on your ticket class and frequent flyer status.
- **Priority Pass Lounges:** If you have a Priority Pass membership, you can access several airport lounges in Fiji, including the Tanoa International Hotel Lounge at Nadi International Airport. Priority Pass membership fees vary depending on the level of access you choose, but they can provide cost-effective access to lounges worldwide.
- **Pacific Island Club Lounge (Nadi International Airport):** The Pacific Island Club Lounge at Nadi International Airport offers comfortable seating, light refreshments, and Wi-Fi access. While prices for access are not publicly available, it may offer more budget-friendly options compared to other lounges at the airport.
- **Day Passes:** Some airport lounges offer day passes that allow travelers to access lounge amenities for a set fee, typically ranging from $25 to $50 USD per person. Check with individual lounges at Nadi International Airport to inquire about day pass availability and pricing.
- **Hotel Packages:** Some hotels near Nadi International Airport offer packages that include access to their airport lounges for guests staying at the hotel. While these packages may not always be the cheapest option, they can provide added value if you're already planning to stay overnight near the airport.

100 useful Fijian phrases with English pronunciation

- Bula! (Boo-lah) - Hello!
- Ni sa bula! (Nee sah boo-lah) - Greetings!
- Moce! (Moh-they) - Goodbye!
- Vinaka! (Vee-nah-kah) - Thank you!
- Vinaka vaka levu! (Vee-nah-kah vah-kah lay-voo) - Thank you very much!
- Yalo vinaka! (Yah-loh vee-nah-kah) - You're welcome!
- Loloma! (Low-loh-mah) - Love!
- Isa lei! (Ee-sah lay) - Oh dear!
- Veilomani! (Vey-loh-mah-nee) - Be healthy!
- Noqu dodomo! (Noh-ng-oh doh-doh-moh) - Excuse me!
- Veilomani! (Vey-loh-mah-nee) - Good health!
- Na noqu vanua! (Nah noh-ng-oo vah-noo-ah) - My country!
- Vakanuinui vinaka! (Vah-kah-noo-ee-noo-ee vee-nah-kah) - Congratulations!
- E dina! (Eh dee-nah) - For real!
- Isa lei! (Ee-sah lay) - Poor thing!
- Qai kana! (Ng-eye kah-nah) - Let's eat!
- Nau votai! (Now voh-tah-ee) - I am hungry!
- Nau malua! (Now mah-loo-ah) - I am tired!
- Veilomani iko! (Vey-loh-mah-nee ee-koh) - Take care!
- Noqu domoni! (Noh-ng-oh doh-moh-nee) - I'm sorry!
- Sa dri yani! (Sah ng-ree yah-nee) - It's raining!
- Sa yawa! (Sah yah-wah) - It's far!
- Sa voleka! (Sah voh-leng-gah) - It's near!
- Sa sega! (Sah seh-ng-gah) - It's not there!
- Lako mada! (Lah-koh mah-dah) - Please go!
- Ni qai lako! (Nee ng-eye lah-koh) - You go now!
- E dau lako mai! (Eh d-ow lah-koh my) - He/she is coming!
- E sa toso yani! (Eh sah toh-soh yah-nee) - It's moving!
- Ni kua mada! (Nee koo-ah mah-dah) - Please stop!
- Cegu mada! (Theng-goo mah-dah) - Please wait!
- Qai sereki! (Ng-eye seh-reh-kee) - Be careful!
- Vaka malua! (Vah-kah mah-loo-ah) - Slow down!
- Sa sega ni yawa! (Sah seh-ng-gah nee yah-wah) - Not far now!
- Sa qai yaco mai! (Sah ng-eye yah-tho my) - Coming soon!
- Yaloyalo vinaka! (Yah-loh-yah-loh vee-nah-kah) - Beautiful garden!
- Lako! (Lah-koh) - Go!
- Lako sara! (Lah-koh sah-rah) - Go ahead!
- Lako mada mai! (Lah-koh mah-dah my) - Please come!
- Sereki! (Seh-reh-kee) - Slow down!
- Lako tu! (Lah-koh too) - Stand up!
- Cavuta na wai! (Tha-voo-tah nah wah-ee) - Fetch the water!
- Toka! (Tong-gah) - Stone!
- Vale ni soso! (Vah-lay nee soh-soh) - Thatch house!
- Niu! (Nee-oo) - Coconut!
- Vesi! (Veh-see) - Ironwood!

- Bure ni bose! (Boo-reh nee boh-seh) - Chief's house!
- Na burenivalu! (Nah boo-reh-nee-vah-loo) - The war house!
- Nai balebale! (Nye bah-leh-bah-leh) - The garden!
- Bili ni batisoni! (Bee-lee nee bah-tee-soh-nee) - The church bell!
- Na i vola ni yaca! (Nah ee vo-lah nee yah-thah) - The name book!
- Na i lavo ni noda! (Nah ee lah-vo nee noh-dah) - Our money!
- Qai mate! (Ng-eye mah-tey) - I'll die!
- Lako vata! (Lah-koh vah-tah) - Let's go together!
- Me vaka noqu dau! (Meh vah-kah noh-ng-oo dow) - Like my son!
- Me bula na bai! (Meh boo-lah nah bah-ee) - May the cow be well!
- Me bula na kau! (Meh boo-lah nah kow) - May the cow be well!
- Me bula na i vola! (Meh boo-lah nah ee vo-lah) - May the book be well!
- Me bula na vale! (Meh boo-lah nah vah-leh) - May the house be well!
- Me bula na vanua! (Meh boo-lah nah vah-noo-ah) - May the land be well!
- Me bula na i matai! (Meh boo-lah nah ee mah-tah-ee) - May the chiefs be well!
- Me bula na i liuliu! (Meh boo-lah nah ee lee-oo-lee-oo) - May the ladies be well!
- Me bula na i taukei! (Meh boo-lah nah ee tau-kay) - May the indigenous people be well!
- Me bula na i turaga! (Meh boo-lah nah ee too-rah-ng

Common complaints

While Fiji is a stunning destination that offers unforgettable experiences, like any other travel destination, tourists may encounter certain common complaints during their visit. Here are some common complaints and potential solutions:

- **Mosquitoes and Bugs:**
- Complaint: Tourists may find mosquitoes and bugs annoying, especially in tropical areas or during certain seasons.
- Solution: Take a moisturer and add citronella and lemongrass to it. Rub it everywhere, top it up every 4 - 6 hours or after swimming. This natural remedy works really well and was developed by the Inca's.
- **High Prices:**
- Solution: Research and book accommodations and activities in advance to take advantage of early booking discounts. Look for budget-friendly options such as guesthouses, homestays, and local eateries. Consider visiting during the off-peak season when prices may be lower.
- **Language Barrier:**
- Solution: Learn some basic Fijian phrases before your trip to facilitate communication. Carry a phrasebook or translation app for assistance. Many Fijians working in tourism speak English, so don't hesitate to ask for help if needed.
- **Weather Conditions:**
- Solution: Check the weather forecast before your trip and be prepared for sudden changes. Pack appropriate clothing and gear, including rain jackets and waterproof bags. Have indoor backup activities planned in case of inclement weather.
- **Island Time Mentality:**
- Solution: Embrace the laid-back island lifestyle and adjust your expectations accordingly. Allow extra time for transportation and activities, and practice patience when waiting for service.

Understanding Fiji

One of the most captivating aspects of Fiji's history is its rich tapestry of ancient legends and mythical beginnings. According to Fijian oral traditions, the islands were inhabited by legendary figures and mythical gods who shaped the landscape and guided the destiny of its people.

One such legend tells of the great chief Lutunasobasoba, who is believed to have led his people from their ancestral homeland to Fiji aboard a magical canoe known as the Kaunitoni. Lutunasobasoba is revered as a divine leader who united the diverse tribes of Fiji under his rule, laying the foundation for the unique cultural heritage of the islands.

Another prominent figure in Fijian mythology is the god Degei, the serpent god of the underworld and creator of the world. According to legend, Degei resides in the depths of the Nakauvadra Mountains, where he guards the sacred waters of life and holds sway over the natural elements.

Colonial Encounters and Cultural Exchange:

The arrival of European explorers in the late 18th century marked a significant turning point in Fiji's history, leading to a period of colonial encounters and cultural exchange. European powers, including Britain and France, vied for control over the islands, attracted by Fiji's strategic location and abundant resources.

The British Empire established colonial rule over Fiji in 1874, following a series of treaties with local chiefs. The colonial period saw the introduction of Western education, governance systems, and economic structures that shaped modern Fijian society. Christianity was also introduced to Fiji by European missionaries, leading to the conversion of many Fijians to Christianity and the establishment of Christian churches across the islands.

Legacy of Indentured Labor:

One of the most significant chapters in Fiji's history is the era of indentured labor, during which thousands of Indian laborers were brought to Fiji to work on sugarcane plantations under British colonial rule. Between 1879 and 1916, over 60,000 Indian laborers, known as "Girmitiyas," were recruited to Fiji under indenture agreements.

The legacy of indentured labor continues to shape Fiji's cultural landscape, contributing to the diversity of its population and the richness of its cultural heritage. Today, descendants of indentured laborers form a significant portion of Fiji's population and have made valuable contributions to the country's social, economic, and cultural development.

Struggle for Independence and Nationhood:

Fiji gained independence from British colonial rule in 1970, marking a significant milestone in the nation's history. The struggle for independence was led by visionary leaders such as Ratu Sir Kamisese Mara and A.D. Patel, who advocated for self-determination and democratic governance.

Since gaining independence, Fiji has navigated its path as a sovereign nation, overcoming challenges such as political instability, ethnic tensions, and coups d'état. The adoption of a republican constitution in 1987 paved the way for Fiji to become a republic within the Commonwealth, with its own indigenous Fijian-led government.

Cultural Resilience and Revival:

Throughout Fiji's history, its people have demonstrated remarkable resilience in the face of adversity, drawing strength from their cultural heritage and sense of community. Despite the challenges of colonialism, indentured labor, and political upheaval, Fijians have preserved and celebrated their traditional customs, languages, and arts.

In recent years, there has been a renewed interest in reviving and preserving Fijian cultural traditions, with initiatives such as cultural festivals, language revitalization programs, and community-based tourism experiences. These efforts reflect a deep-seated pride in Fijian identity and a commitment to honoring the legacy of ancestors who have shaped the nation's history.

Tourists' Fascination with Fijian History:

Tourists visiting Fiji are often fascinated by the depth and complexity of its history, which is woven into the fabric of everyday life on the islands. From exploring ancient archaeological sites to immersing themselves in vibrant cultural festivals, visitors have countless opportunities to engage with Fiji's rich historical heritage.

Many tourists are drawn to Fiji's ancient legends and mythical narratives, which provide a captivating glimpse into the beliefs and traditions of its indigenous peoples. Others are intrigued by the legacy of colonialism and indentured labor, which has left indelible marks on Fiji's cultural landscape and shaped its contemporary identity.

Moreover, tourists are often inspired by the resilience and determination of the Fijian people, who have overcome adversity with grace and perseverance. By learning about Fiji's history, visitors gain a deeper appreciation for the cultural diversity, social dynamics, and enduring traditions that make these islands so unique.

Understanding the mindset of the average Fijian requires delving into the cultural values, societal norms, and historical context that shape their worldview. While individual perspectives may vary, there are some common themes that offer insight into the Fijian mindset.

Community-Centric Values: Fijian society is deeply rooted in communal living, where the well-being of the community takes precedence over individual interests. The concept of "vanua" (land and people) underscores the interconnectedness of Fijians with their land, culture, and each other. As a result, cooperation, mutual support, and respect for elders are highly valued.

Spirituality and Tradition: Religion plays a significant role in the lives of many Fijians, with Christianity being the dominant faith. Traditional Fijian spirituality also coexists alongside Christianity, manifesting in rituals, ceremonies, and beliefs centered around ancestral worship and connection to the land. These spiritual beliefs often shape Fijians' outlook on life, guiding their actions and decisions.

Resilience and Adaptability: Fijians are known for their resilience in the face of adversity, stemming from a history marked by colonialism, natural disasters, and socio-economic challenges. Despite these hardships, Fijians maintain a strong sense of optimism, resourcefulness, and adaptability, drawing strength from their cultural heritage and community bonds.

Hospitality and Generosity: Fijians are renowned for their warm hospitality and generosity towards visitors and guests. The practice of "bulasali" (sharing with others) is deeply ingrained in Fijian culture, where guests are welcomed with open arms and treated like family. This spirit of generosity fosters strong social connections and fosters a sense of belonging within the community.

As for local jokes, Fijians have a rich tradition of humor and wit, often poking fun at themselves, their cultural quirks, and everyday life. Here are a few lighthearted jokes commonly heard in Fiji:

- Why did the Fijian bring a ladder to the bar? Because he heard the drinks were on the house!
- How many Fijians does it take to change a lightbulb? None, they'll just sit back and enjoy the darkness!

Checklist of the top 20 things to do in Fiji

✅ Explore the Coral Reefs: Dive or snorkel among vibrant coral reefs teeming with marine life.

✅ Visit Tavoro Waterfalls: Hike through lush rainforest to reach the stunning Tavoro Waterfalls in Bouma National Heritage Park.

✅ Relax on Natadola Beach: Sink your toes into the soft white sand of Natadola Beach, one of Fiji's most picturesque beaches.

✅ Experience a Kava Ceremony: Participate in a traditional Fijian kava ceremony, where you'll drink the mildly sedative kava root infusion.

✅ Cruise the Yasawa Islands: Embark on a cruise through the pristine waters of the Yasawa Islands, stopping at secluded beaches and remote villages.

✅ Discover Sabeto Hot Springs: Soak in the natural thermal pools of Sabeto Hot Springs and Mud Pools for a rejuvenating experience.

✅ Visit the Sri Siva Subramaniya Temple: Explore the colorful Sri Siva Subramaniya Temple, the largest Hindu temple in the Southern Hemisphere.

✅ Go Zip-lining in Pacific Harbour: Experience an adrenaline rush as you zip-line through the lush rainforest canopy in Pacific Harbour.

✅ Explore the Garden of the Sleeping Giant: Wander through the botanical wonderland of the Garden of the Sleeping Giant, home to exotic orchids and lush tropical foliage.

✅ Dive with Bull Sharks: Brave a thrilling dive with bull sharks in the Beqa Lagoon for an unforgettable underwater adventure.

✅ Take a Sigatoka River Safari: Embark on a scenic cruise along the Sigatoka River, passing through pristine mangrove forests and traditional Fijian villages.

✅ Visit the Fiji Museum: Immerse yourself in Fiji's history and culture at the Fiji Museum, home to artifacts, exhibits, and traditional Fijian crafts.

✅ Explore Levuka Historical Port Town: Step back in time as you wander through the historic streets of Levuka, Fiji's first capital and a UNESCO World Heritage Site.

✅ Relax in the Sabeto Valley: Unwind in the tranquil surroundings of the Sabeto Valley, known for its natural beauty and therapeutic hot springs.

✅ Dive the Rainbow Reef: Dive the technicolor depths of the Rainbow Reef, renowned for its vibrant coral formations and diverse marine life.

✅ Experience Fijian Village Life: Gain insight into traditional Fijian culture and customs with a visit to a local village, where you can participate in cultural activities and interact with villagers.

✅ Enjoy a Sunset Cruise: Set sail on a sunset cruise along Fiji's pristine coastline, sipping cocktails and soaking in the breathtaking views.

✅ Hike to the Summit of Mount Tomanivi: Challenge yourself with a hike to the summit of Mount Tomanivi, Fiji's highest peak, for panoramic views of the surrounding landscape.

✅ Indulge in a Fijian Lovo Feast: Feast on a traditional Fijian lovo feast, where food is cooked in an underground oven for a mouthwatering culinary experience.

✅ Go Cave Exploring in the Sawa-i-Lau Caves: Venture into the mystical depths of the Sawa-i-Lau Caves, where you can swim in underground pools and marvel at ancient rock formations.

Money Mistakes

Money Mistake	How to Avoid It
Overlooking Hidden Fees	Read the fine print and ask about any additional fees or taxes before booking accommodations, tours, or activities. Budget for these expenses to avoid surprises during your trip.
Exchanging Currency at Airport	Avoid exchanging currency at the airport, as rates tend to be less favorable. Instead, withdraw Fijian dollars from ATMs or use credit cards with no foreign transaction fees for better rates.
Falling for Tourist Traps	Research and compare prices for tours, activities, and souvenirs to avoid overpaying for tourist traps. Seek recommendations from locals or fellow travelers for authentic and budget-friendly experiences.
Ignoring Bargaining Opportunities	Don't be afraid to negotiate prices in local markets or with independent vendors. Polite bargaining is common in Fiji and can result in significant savings on souvenirs, tours, and transportation.

Recap chart: How to have a $5,000 trip to Fiji for just $500

Aspect	Original Cost	Cost-Saving Tips
Accommodation	$200	- Utilize dorms in resorts or day passes to luxury hotels for access to amenities without the overnight cost. Look for discounted rates during off-peak seasons. Consider staying in budget-friendly guesthouses or hostels.
Transportation	$100	- Use ferries for inter-island travel instead of expensive flights. Opt for public buses for inland transportation. Book transportation in advance for the best deals.
Food & Dining	$100	- Indulge in street eats and local markets for authentic and affordable cuisine. Look for meal deals at restaurants and eateries frequented by locals.
Activities & Excursions	$100	- Research free or low-cost activities such as hiking, beachcombing, and snorkeling. Take advantage of complimentary amenities offered by accommodations. Look for discounted excursions or group rates.
Total		**$500**

Total: $500

By following these budget-friendly tips and recommendations, you can enjoy a fantastic trip to Fiji for just $500, allowing you to experience the beauty and culture of the islands without breaking the bank. Remember to plan ahead, research discounts, and prioritize your spending to make the most of your budget-friendly adventure in Fiji!

Practical Tips to Remember

Take Advantage of Happy Hours:

Specifics: Look for bars and restaurants that offer happy hour specials, typically in the late afternoon or early evening. Enjoy discounted prices on drinks and food items, such as cocktails, beer, wine, and appetizers.

Example: Head to The Rhum-Ba at Port Denarau, which offers happy hour specials from 4 PM to 6 PM daily, with discounts on selected drinks and bar snacks.

Explore Free Attractions:

Specifics: Seek out free natural attractions such as Saweni Beach in Lautoka, Tavoro Waterfalls in Taveuni, and the Sigatoka Sand Dunes National Park. These destinations offer opportunities for swimming, hiking, and sightseeing without any entrance fees.

Example: Visit the Sabeto Hot Springs and Mud Pool near Nadi, where you can enjoy natural thermal pools and therapeutic mud baths for free, with optional spa treatments available at an additional cost.

Use Local Transport Options:

Take a local bus from Suva to Colo-i-Suva Forest Park for just a few Fijian dollars, where you can hike through lush rainforest trails and swim in refreshing natural pools.

Take Advantage of Free Activities:

Specifics: Look for free or low-cost activities such as attending traditional meke performances, where you can experience Fijian music, dance, and storytelling. Join beach cleanups organized by local conservation groups to contribute to environmental preservation while meeting like-minded travelers.

Example: Participate in a free cultural demonstration at the Arts Village in Pacific Harbour, where you can learn traditional Fijian crafts such as weaving and woodcarving.

Enjoy Day Passes to Luxury Resorts:

Specifics: Look for luxury resorts in Fiji that offer day passes to non-guests. These passes typically grant access to resort amenities such as pools, beaches, and fitness centers, as well as discounts on spa treatments and dining options.

Example: Purchase a day pass for the InterContinental Fiji Golf Resort & Spa, which includes access to the resort's stunning pool complex, beachfront facilities, and discounted rates on spa treatments and dining.

Consider Volunteer Experiences:

Specifics: Research volunteer opportunities with local organizations or conservation projects in Fiji. In exchange for your volunteer work, you may receive complimentary accommodation, meals, and cultural experiences, allowing you to immerse yourself in the local community while stretching your budget.

Example: Volunteer with a marine conservation organization like GVI Fiji, where you can participate in coral reef monitoring, marine research, and community outreach programs. In return, you may receive free accommodation in a volunteer house and meals.

Off-the-Beaten-Path Activities: Seek out off-the-beaten-path activities and attractions that are free or low-cost. Explore hidden waterfalls, hike scenic trails, or snorkel in secluded bays away from the tourist crowds. You'll have a more authentic experience while saving money on expensive tours and activities. Potential Savings: Hundreds of dollars.

Travel During Shoulder Seasons: Take advantage of shoulder seasons, the periods between peak and off-peak seasons, to score deals on flights, accommodation, and activities. You'll enjoy lower prices and fewer crowds while still experiencing Fiji's beautiful weather and attractions. Potential Savings: Hundreds of dollars.

Negotiate Prices: Don't be afraid to negotiate prices for goods and services, especially in local markets and with independent vendors. Polite bargaining is common in Fiji and can result in significant savings on souvenirs, tours, and transportation. Potential Savings: Dozens of dollars.

Strategies for the best trip

1. Embrace Fiji Time: The Island's Relaxed Pace

Get ready to unwind and adjust your clock to "Fiji Time." Islanders operate on a more relaxed schedule, so don't be surprised if things move a bit slower than you're used to. This laid-back attitude is part of Fiji's charm, so embrace it and let yourself fully relax into the island vibe.

2. Respect Local Customs: Cover Up in Villages

When visiting Fijian villages, it's essential to dress modestly out of respect for local customs. This means covering your shoulders and knees, especially when entering sacred sites or participating in traditional ceremonies. Pack lightweight, breathable clothing like sarongs or maxi dresses to stay cool while adhering to cultural norms.

3. Pack Reef-Safe Sunscreen: Protect the Marine Life

Fiji boasts stunning coral reefs and marine ecosystems, so it's crucial to protect them while enjoying the sun and sea. Opt for reef-safe sunscreen brands that are free of harmful chemicals like oxybenzone and octinoxate, which can damage coral reefs and marine life. Look for mineral-based sunscreens with ingredients like zinc oxide or titanium dioxide to ensure your skin stays protected without harming the environment.

4. Stay Hydrated: Beat the Heat with Coconut Water

Fiji can get hot and humid, especially during the summer months, so it's essential to stay hydrated throughout your trip. Embrace the local tradition of drinking fresh coconut water straight from the source. Not only is it refreshing and delicious, but it's also packed with electrolytes to keep you hydrated and energized under the tropical sun.

5. Learn Basic Fijian Phrases: Connect with Locals

While English is widely spoken in Fiji, learning a few basic Fijian phrases can go a long way in connecting with locals and showing respect for the culture. Practice greetings like "Bula" (hello) and "Vinaka" (thank you), and don't be afraid to engage with Fijians in their native language. Your efforts will be appreciated and warmly received by the local community.

6. Explore Beyond the Resorts: Discover Hidden Gems

While Fiji's luxury resorts offer comfort and convenience, don't miss out on exploring the island's lesser-known treasures. Venture beyond the tourist hotspots to discover hidden gems like secluded beaches, lush rainforests, and charming villages. Rent a car or hire a local guide to explore off-the-beaten-path destinations and immerse yourself in the authentic beauty of Fiji.

9. Tipping is Not Expected: Appreciate the No-Tipping Culture

Unlike some Western countries, tipping is not expected or customary in Fiji. While it's always appreciated to reward exceptional service, it's not obligatory, and locals don't expect gratuities as part of their income. Instead of tipping, show your appreciation by offering genuine thanks and acknowledging good service with a warm smile and friendly demeanor.

10. Take Cash: Credit Cards Aren't Always Accepted

While major credit cards are accepted at most hotels, restaurants, and tourist attractions in Fiji, it's always a good idea to carry cash for small purchases and transactions. Some smaller shops, markets, and street vendors may only accept cash, so having Fijian dollars on hand will ensure you're prepared for any situation. Be sure to visit a local bank or currency exchange to obtain Fijian currency upon arrival.

11. Protect Your Valuables: Use Waterproof Bags

Fiji's pristine beaches and crystal-clear waters beckon for swimming, snorkeling, and water sports, but they also pose a risk to your belongings. Protect your valuables from water damage by investing in waterproof bags or dry pouches to keep your phone, camera, and other electronics safe and dry while you enjoy the ocean. These handy accessories are a lifesaver for beach lovers and water enthusiasts alike.

The secret to saving HUGE amounts of money when travelling to Fiji is...

Your mindset. Money is an emotional topic, if you associate words like cheapskate, Miser with being thrifty when traveling you are likely to say 'F-it' and spend your money needlessly because you associate pain with saving money. You pay now for an immediate reward. Our brains are prehistoric; they focus on surviving day to day. Travel companies and hotels know this and put trillions into making you believe you will be happier when you spend on their products or services. Our poor brains are up against outdated programming and an onslaught of advertisements bombarding us with the message: spending money on travel equals PLEASURE. To correct this carefully lodged propaganda in your frontal cortex, you need to imagine your future self.

Saving money does not make you a cheapskate. It makes you smart. How do people get rich? They invest their money. They don't go out and earn it; they let their money earn more money. So every time you want to spend money, imagine this: while you travel, your money is working for you, not you for money. While you sleep, the money, you've invested is going up and up. That's a pleasure a pricey entrance fee can't give you. Thinking about putting your money to work for you tricks your brain into believing you are not withholding pleasure from yourself, you are saving your money to invest so you can go to even more amazing places. You are thus turning thrifty travel into a pleasure fueled sport.

When you've got money invested - If you want to splash your cash on a first-class airplane seat - you can. I can't tell you how to invest your money, only that you should. Saving $20 on taxis doesn't seem like much, but over time you could save upwards of $15,000 a year, which is a deposit for a house which you can rent on Airbnb to finance more travel. Your brain making money looks like your brain on cocaine, so tell yourself saving money is making money.

Scientists have proved that imagining your future self is the easiest way to associate pleasure with saving money. You can download FaceApp — which will give you a picture of what you will look like older and grayer, or you can take a deep breath just before spending money and ask yourself if you will regret the purchase later.

The easiest ways to waste money traveling are:

Getting a taxi. The solution to this is to always download the google map before you go. Many taxi drivers will drive you around for 15 minutes when the place you were trying to get to is a 5-minute walk... remember while not getting an overpriced taxi to tell yourself, 'I am saving money to free myself for more travel.'
Spending money on overpriced food when hungry. The solution: carry snacks. A banana and an apple will cost you, in most places, less than a dollar.

Spending on entrance fees to top-rated attractions. If you really want to do it, spend the money happily. If you're conflicted, sleep on it. I don't regret spending $200 on a sky dive over the Great Barrier Reef; I regret going to the top of the shard on a cloudy day in Fiji for $60. Only you can know, but make sure it's your decision and not the marketing directors at said top-rated attraction.

Telling yourself 'you only have the chance to see/eat/experience it now'. While this might be true, make sure YOU WANT to spend the money. Money spent is money you can't invest, and often you can have the same experience for much less.

You can experience luxurious travel on a small budget, which will trick your brain into thinking you're already a high-roller, which will mean you'll be more likely to act like one and invest your money. Stay in five-star hotels for $5 by booking on the day of your stay on booking.com to enjoy last-minute deals. You can go to fancy restaurants using daily deal sites. Ask your airline about last-minute upgrades to first-class or business. I paid $100 extra on a $179 ticket to Cuba from Germany to be bumped to Business Class. When you ask, it will surprise you what you can get both at hotels and airlines.

Travel, as the saying goes, is the only thing you spend money on that makes you richer. You can easily waste money, making it difficult to enjoy that metaphysical wealth. The biggest money saving secret is to turn bargain hunting into a pleasurable activity, not an annoyance. Budgeting consciously can be fun, don't feel disappointed because you don't spend the $60 to go into an attraction. Feel good because soon that $60 will soon earn money for you. Meaning, you'll have the time and money to enjoy more metaphysical wealth while your bank balance increases.

So there it is. You can save a small fortune by being strategic with your trip planning. We've arranged everything in the guide to offer the best bang for your buck. Which means we took the view that if it's not an excellent investment for your money, we wouldn't include it. Why would a guide called 'Super Cheap' include lots of overpriced attractions? That said, if you think we've missed something or have unanswered questions, ping me an email: philgtang@gmail.com I'm on central Europe time and usually reply within 8 hours of getting your mail. We like to think of our guide books as evolving organisms helping our readers travel better cheaper. We use reader questions via email to update this book year round so you'll be helping other readers and yourself.

Don't put your dreams off!

Time is a currency you never get back and travel is its greatest return on investment. Plus, now you know you can visit Fiji for a fraction of the price most would have you believe.

Thank you for reading

Dear **Lovely Reader**,

If you have found this book useful, please consider writing a quick review on Online Retailers.

One person from every 1000 readers leaves a review on Online Retailers. It would mean more than you could ever know if you were one of our 1 in 1000 people to take the time to write a brief review.

Thank you so much for reading again and for spending your time and investing your trips future in Super Cheap Insider Guides.

One last note, please don't listen to anyone who says 'Oh no, you can't visit Fiji on a budget'. Unlike you, they didn't have this book. You can do ANYWHERE on a budget with the right insider advice and planning. Sure, learning to travel to Fiji on a budget that doesn't compromise on anything or drastically compromise on safety or comfort levels is a skill, but this guide has done the detective work for you. Now it is time for you to put the advice into action.

Phil and the Super Cheap Insider Guides Team

P.S If you need any more super cheap tips we'd love to hear from you e-mail me at philgtang@gmail.com, we have a lot of contacts in every region, so if there's a specific bargain you're hunting we can help you find it.

DISCOVER YOUR NEXT VACATION

☑ **LUXURY ON A BUDGET APPROACH**
☑ **CHOOSE FROM 107 DESTINATIONS**
☑ **EACH BOOK PACKED WITH REAL-TIME LOCAL TIPS**

All are available in Paperback and e-book on Online Retailers:
https://www.Online Retailers.com/dp/B09C2DHQG5

Several are available as audiobooks. You can watch excerpts of ALL for FREE on YouTube: https://youtube.com/channel/UCxo9YV8-M9P1cFosU-Gjnqg

COUNTRY GUIDES

Super Cheap AUSTRALIA
Super Cheap CANADA
Super Cheap DENMARK
Super Cheap FINLAND
Super Cheap FRANCE
Super Cheap GERMANY
Super Cheap ICELAND
Super Cheap IRELAND
Super Cheap JAPAN
Super Cheap LUXEMBOURG
Super Cheap MALDIVES 2024
Super Cheap NEW ZEALAND
Super Cheap NORWAY
Super Cheap SPAIN
Super Cheap SWITZERLAND

MORE GUIDES

Super Cheap ADELAIDE 2024
Super Cheap ALASKA 2024
Super Cheap AUSTIN 2024
Super Cheap BANGKOK 2024
Super Cheap BARCELONA 2024
Super Cheap BELFAST 2024
Super Cheap BERMUDA 2024
Super Cheap BORA BORA 2024
Super Cheap Great Barrier Reef 2024
Super Cheap CAMBRIDGE 2024
Super Cheap CANCUN 2024
Super Cheap CHIANG MAI 2024
Super Cheap CHICAGO 2024
Super Cheap DOHA 2024
Super Cheap DUBAI 2024

Super Cheap DUBLIN 2024
Super Cheap EDINBURGH 2024
Super Cheap GALWAY 2024
Super Cheap LAS VEGAS 2024
Super Cheap LIMA 2024
Super Cheap LISBON 2024
Super Cheap MALAGA 2024
Super Cheap Machu Pichu 2024
Super Cheap MIAMI 2024
Super Cheap Milan 2024
Super Cheap NASHVILLE 2024
Super Cheap NEW ORLEANS 2024
Super Cheap NEW YORK 2024
Super Cheap PARIS 2024
Super Cheap SEYCHELLES 2024
Super Cheap SINGAPORE 2024
Super Cheap ST LUCIA 2024
Super Cheap TORONTO 2024
Super Cheap TURKS AND CAICOS 2024
Super Cheap VENICE 2024
Super Cheap VIENNA 2024
Super Cheap YOSEMITE 2024
Super Cheap ZURICH 2024
Super Cheap ZANZIBAR 2024

Bonus Travel Hacks

I've included these bonus travel hacks to help you plan and enjoy your trip to Fiji cheaply, joyfully, and smoothly. Perhaps they will even inspire you to start or renew a passion for long-term travel.

Common pitfalls when it comes to allocating money to your desires while traveling

Beware of Malleable mental accounting

Let's say you budgeted spending only $30 per day in Fiji but then you say well if I was at home I'd be spending $30 on food as an everyday purchase so you add another $30 to your budget. Don't fall into that trap as the likelihood is you still have expenses at home even if its just the cost of keeping your freezer going.

Beware of impulse purchases in Fiji

Restaurants that you haven't researched and just idle into can sometimes turn out to be great, but more often, they turn out to suck, especially if they are near tourist attractions. Make yourself a travel itinerary including where you'll eat breakfast and lunch. Dinner is always more expensive, so the meal best to enjoy at home or as a takeaway. This book is full of incredible cheap eats. All you have to do is plan to go to them.

Social media and FOMO (Fear of Missing Out)

'The pull of seeing acquaintances spend money on travel can often be a more powerful motivator to spend more while traveling than seeing an advertisement.' Beware of what you allow to influence you and go back to the question, what's the best money I can spend today?

Now-or-never sales strategies

One reason tourists are targeted by salespeople is the success of the now-or-never strategy. If you don't spend the money now... your never get the opportunity again. Rarely is this true.

Instead of spending your money on something you might not actually desire, take five minutes. Ask yourself, do I really want this? And return to the answer in five minutes. Your body will either say an absolute yes with a warm, excited feeling or a no with a weak, obscure feeling.

Unexpected costs

"Holding on to anger is like grasping a hot coal with the intent of throwing it at someone else; you only hurt yourself." The Buddha.

One downside to traveling is unexpected costs. When these spring up from airlines, accommodation providers, tours and on and on, they feel like a punch in the gut. During the pandemic my earnings fell to 20% of what they are normally. No one was traveling, no one was buying travel guides. My accountant out of nowhere significantly raised his fee for the year despite the fact there was a lot less money to count. I was so angry I consulted a lawyer who told me you will spend more taking him to court than you will paying his bill. I had to get myself into a good feeling place before I paid his bill, so I googled how to feel good paying someone who has scammed you.

The answer: Write down that you will receive 10 times the amount you are paying from an unexpected source. I did that. Four months later, the accountant wrote to me. He had applied for a COVID subsidy for me and I would receive… you guessed it almost exactly 10 times his fee.

Make of that what you want. I don't wish to get embroiled in a conversation about what many term 'woo-woo', but the result of my writing that I would receive 10 times the amount made me feel much, much better when paying him. And ultimately, that was a gift in itself. So next time some airline or train operator or hotel/ Airbnb sticks you with an unexpected fee, immediately write that you will receive 10 times the amount you are paying from an unexpected source. Rise your vibe and skip the added price of feeling angry.

Hack your allocations for your Fiji Trip

"The best trick for saving is to eliminate the decision to save." Perry Wright of Duke University.

Put the money you plan to spend in Fiji on a pre-paid card in the local currency. This cuts out two problems - not knowing how much you've spent and totally avoiding expensive currency conversion fees.

You could even create separate spaces. This much for transportation, this for tours/ entertainment, accommodation and food. We are reluctant to spend money that is pre-assigned to categories or uses.

Write that you want to enjoy a $3,000 trip for $500 to your Fiji trip. Countless research shows when you put goals in writing, you have a higher chance of following through.

Spend all the money you want to on buying experiences in Fiji

"Experiences are like good relatives that stay for a while and then leave. Objects are like relatives who move in and stay past their welcome." Daniel Gilbert, psychologist from Harvard University.

Economic and psychological research shows we are happier buying brief experiences on vacation rather than buying stuff to wear so give yourself freedom to spend on experiences knowing that the value you get back is many many times over.

Make saving money a game

There's one day a year where all the thrift shops where me and my family live sell everything there for a $1. My wife and I hold a contest where we take $5 and buy an entire outfit for each other. Whoever's outfit is liked more wins. We also look online to see whose outfit would have cost more to buy new. This year, my wife even snagged me an Armani coat for $1. I liked the coat when she showed it to me, but when I found out it was $500 new; I liked it and wore it a lot more.

Quadruple your money

Every-time you want to spend money, imagine it quadrupled. So the $10 you want to spend is actually $40. Now imagine that what you want to buy is four times the price. Do you still want it? If yes, go enjoy. If not, you've just saved yourself money, know you can choose to invest it in a way that quadruples or allocate it to something you really want to give you a greater return.

Understand what having unlimited amounts of money to spend in Fiji actually looks like

Let's look at what it would be like to have unlimited amounts of money to spend on your trip to Fiji.

Isolation

You take a private jet to your private Fiji hotel. There you are lavished with the best food, drink, and entertainment. Spending vast amounts of money on vacation equals being isolated.

Expense Category	Typical Cost ($5,000 Trip)	Budget-Friendly Tips & Recommendations ($500 Trip)
Accommodation	$200	Stay in budget accommodations such as, dorms within resorts, guesthouses, or Airbnb. Look for discounts or promotions, and consider shared accommodations or camping for even lower costs and visit luxury resorts with day passes.
Food	$100	Eat at local eateries, markets, and street food stalls for affordable meals. Cook your meals using local ingredients, and opt for self-catering accommodations to save on dining expenses.
Transportation	$100	Utilize public transportation, such as buses or shared taxis, instead of private transfers. Walk or bike whenever possible to explore the area. Look for discounted transportation passes or group tours. Use Ferries to explore islands and stay in accommodation with free transfers for one night before you travel to save on ferry costs.
Activities & Excursions	$100	Choose free or low-cost activities such as hiking, swimming, or exploring cultural sites. Look for discounted or off-peak tours and attractions. Take advantage of complimentary activities offered by accommodations.

If you're on your honeymoon and you want to be alone with your Amore, this is wonderful, but it can be equally wonderful to make new friends. Know this a study 'carried out by Brigham Young University, Utah found that while obesity increased risk of death by 30%, loneliness increased it by half.'

Comfort

Money can buy you late check outs of five-star hotels and priority boarding on airlines, all of which add up to comfort. But as this book has shown you, saving money in Fiji doesn't minimize comfort, that's just a lie travel agencies littered with glossy brochures want you to believe.

You can do late-check outs for free with the right credit cards and priority boarding can be purchased with a lot of airlines from $4. If you want to go big with first-class or business, flights offset your own travel costs by renting your own home or you can upgrade at the airport often for a fraction of what you would have paid booking a business flight online.

MORE TIPS TO FIND CHEAP FLIGHTS

“The use of travelling is to regulate imagination by reality, and instead of thinking how thin gs may be, to see them as they are.” Samuel Jackson

If you’re working full-time, you can save yourself a lot of money by requesting your time off from work starting in the middle of the week. Tuesdays and Wednesdays are the cheapest days to fly. You can save thousands just by adjusting your time off.

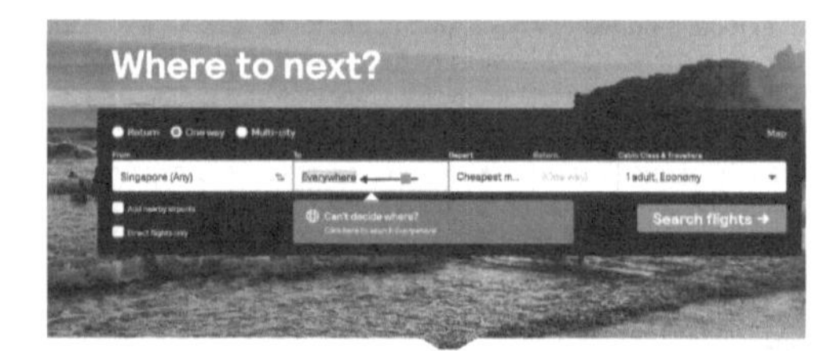

The simplest secret to booking cheap flights is open parameters. Let’s say you want to fly from Chicago to Paris. You enter the USA in from and select Fiji under to. You may find flights from New York City to Paris for $70. Then you just need to find a cheap flight to NYC. Make sure you calculate full costs, including if you need airport accommodation and of course getting to and from airports, **but in nearly every instance open parameters will save you at least half the cost of the flight.**

If you’re not sure about where you want to go, use open parameters to show you the cheapest destinations from your city. Start with skyscanner.net they include the low-cost airlines that others like Kayak leave out. Google Flights can also show you cheap destinations. To see these leave the WHERE TO section blank. Open parameters can also show you the cheapest dates to fly. If you’re flexible, you can save up to 80% of the flight cost. Always check the weather at your destination before you book. Sometimes a $400 flight will be $20, because it’s monsoon season. But hey, if you like the rain, why not?

ALWAYS USE A PRIVATE BROWSER TO BOOK FLIGHTS

Skyscanner and other sites track your IP address and put prices up and down based on what they determine your strength of conviction to buy. e.g. if you’ve booked one-way and are looking for the return, these sites will jack the prices up by in most cases 50%. Incognito browsing pays.

Use a VPN such as Hola to book your flight from your destination

Install Hola, change your destination to the country you are flying to. The location from which a ticket is booked can affect the price significantly as algorithms consider local buying power.

Choose the right time to buy your ticket.

Choose the right time to buy your ticket, as purchasing tickets on a Sunday has been proven to be cheaper. If you can only book during the week, try to do it on a Tuesday.

Mistake fares

Email alerts from individual carriers are where you can find the best 'mistake fares". This is where a computer error has resulted in an airline offering the wrong fare. In my experience, it's best to sign up to individual carriers email lists, but if you ARE lazy Secret Flying puts together a daily roster of mistake fares. Visit https://www.secretflying.com/errorfare/ to see if there're any errors that can benefit you.

Fly late for cheaper prices

Red-eye flights, the ones that leave later in the day, are typically cheaper and less crowded, so aim to book that flight if possible. You will also get through the airport much quicker at the end of the day. Just make sure there's ground transport available for when you land. You don't want to save $50 on the airfare and spend it on a taxi to your accommodation.

Use this APP for same day flights

If your plans are flexible, use 'Get The Flight Out' (http://www.gtfoflights.com/) a fare tracker Hopper that shows you same-day deeply discounted flights. This is best for long-haul flights with major carriers. You can often find a British Airways round-trip from JFK Airport to Heathrow for $300. If you booked this in advance, you'd pay at least double.

Take an empty water bottle with you

Airport prices on food and drinks are sky high. It disgusts me to see some airports charging $10 for a bottle of water. ALWAYS take an empty water bottle with you. It's relatively unknown, but most airports have drinking water fountains past the security check. Just type in your airport name to wateratairports.com to locate the fountain. Then once you've passed security (because they don't allow you to take 100ml or more of liquids) you can freely refill your bottle with water.

Round-the-World (RTW) Tickets

It is always cheaper to book your flights using a DIY approach. First, you may decide you want to stay longer in one country, and a RTW will charge you a hefty fee for changing your flight. Secondly, it all depends on where and when you travel and as we have discussed, there are many ways to ensure you pay way less than $1,500 for a year of flights. If you're travelling long-haul, the best strategy is to buy a return ticket, say New York, to Bangkok and then take cheap flights or transport around Asia and even to Australia and beyond.

Cut your costs to and from airports

Don't you hate it when getting to and from the airport is more expensive than your flight! And this is true in so many cities, especially European ones. For some reason, Google often shows the most expensive options. Use Omio to compare the cheapest transport options and save on airport transfer costs.

Car sharing instead of taxis

Check if Fiji has car sharing at the airport. Often they'll be tons of cars parked at the airport that are half the price of taking a taxi into the city. In most instances, you register your driving licence on an app and scan the code on the car to get going.

Checking Bags

Sometimes you need to check bags. If you do, put an AirTag inside. That way, you'll be about to see when you land where your bag is. This saves you the nail biting wait at baggage claim. And if worse comes to worst, and you see your bag is actually in another city, you can calmly stroll over to customer services and show them where your bag is.

Is it cheaper and more convenient to send your bags ahead?

Before you check your bags, check if it's cheaper to send them ahead of you with sendmybag.com obviously if you're staying in an Airbnb, you'll need to ask the hosts permission or you can time them to arrive the day after you. Hotels are normally very amenable.

What Credit Card Gives The Best Air Miles?

You can slash the cost of flights just for spending on a piece of plastic.

LET'S TALK ABOUT DEBT

Before we go into the best cards for each country, let's first talk about debt. The US system offers the best and biggest rewards. Why? Because they rely on the fact that many people living in the US will not pay their cards in full and the card will earn the bank significant interest payments. Other countries have a very different attitude towards money, debt, and saving than Americans. Thus in Germany and Austria the offerings aren't as favourable as the UK, Fiji and Australia, where debt culture is more widely embraced. The takeaway here is this: **Only spend on one of these cards when you have set-up an automatic total monthly balance repayment. Don't let banks profit from your lizard brain!**

The best air-mile credit cards for those living in the UK

Amex Preferred Rewards Gold comes out top for those living in the UK for 2024.

Here are the benefits:

- 20,000-point bonus on £3,000 spend in first three months. These can be used towards flights with British Airways, Virgin Atlantic, Emirates and Etihad, and often other rewards, such as hotel stays and car hire.
- 1 point per £1 spent
- 1 point = 1 airline point
- Two free visits a year to airport lounges
- No fee in year one, then £140/yr

The downside:

- Fail to repay fully and it's 59.9% rep APR interest, incl fee

You'll need to cancel before the £140/yr fee kicks in year two if you want to avoid it.

The best air-mile credit cards for those living in Canada

Aeroplan is the superior rewards program in Canada. The card has a high earn rate for Aeroplan Points, generating 1.5 points per $1 spent on eligible purchases. Look at the specifics of the eligible purchases https://www.aircanada.com/ca/en/aco/home/aeroplan/earn.html. If you're not spending on these things AMEX's Membership Rewards program offers you the best returns in Canada.

The best air-mile credit cards for those living in Germany

If you have a German bank account, you can apply for a Lufthansa credit card.

Earn 50,000 award miles if you spend $3,000 in purchases and paying the annual fee, both within the first 90 days.

Earn 2 award miles per $1 spent on ticket purchases directly from Miles & More integrated airline partners.

Earn 1 award mile per $1 spent on all other purchases.

The downsides

the €89 annual fee

Limited to fly with Lufthansa and its partners but you can capitalise on perks like the companion pass and airport lounge vouchers.

You need excellent credit to get this card.

The best air-mile credit cards for those living in Austria

"In Austria, Miles & More offers you a special credit card. You get miles for each purchase with the credit card. The Miles & More program calculates miles earned based on the distance flown and booking class. For European flights, the booking class is a flat rate. For intercontinental flights, mileage is calculated by multiplying the booking class by the distance flown." They offer a calculator so you can see how many points you could earn: https://www.miles-and-more.com/at/en/earn/airlines/mileage-calculator.html

The best air-mile credit cards for those living in Fiji:

"The American Express card is the best known and oldest to earn miles, thanks to its membership Rewards program. When making payments with this card, points are added, which can then be exchanged for miles from airlines such as Iberia, Air Europa, Emirates or Alitalia." More information is available here: https://www.americanexpress.com/es-es/

The best air-mile credit cards for those living in Australia

ANZ Rewards Black comes out top for 2024.

180,000 bonus ANZ Reward Points (can get an $800 gift card) and $0 annual fee for the first year with the ANZ Rewards Black
Points Per Spend: 1 Velocity point on purchases of up to $5,000 per statement period and 0.5 Velocity points thereafter.
Annual Fee: $0 in the first year, then $375 after.
Ns no set minimum income required, however, there is a minimum credit limit of $15,000 on this card.

Here are some ways you can hack points onto this card: https://www.pointhacks.com.au/credit-cards/anz-rewards-black-guide/

The best air-mile credit card solution for those living in the USA with a POOR credit score

The downside to Airline Mile cards is that they require good or excellent credit scores, meaning 690 or higher.

If you have bad credit and want to use credit card air lines you will need to rebuild your credit poor. The Credit One Bank® Platinum Visa® for Rebuilding Credit is a good credit card for people with bad credit who don't want to place a deposit on a secured card. The Credit One Platinum Visa offers a $300 credit limit, rewards, and the potential for credit-limit increases, which in time will help rebuild your score.

PLEASE don't sign-up for any of these cards if you can't trust yourself to repay it in full monthly. This will only lead to stress for you.

Frequent Flyer Memberships

"Points" and "miles" are often used interchangeably, but they're usually two very different things. Maximise and diversify your rewards by utilising both.

A frequent-flyer program (FFP) is a loyalty program offered by an airline. They are designed to encourage airline customers to fly more to accumulate points (also called miles, kilometres, or segments) which can be redeemed for air travel or other rewards.

You can sign up with any FFP program for free. There are three major airline alliances in the world: Oneworld, SkyTeam and Star Alliance. I am with One World https://www.oneworld.com/members because the points can be accrued and used for most flights.

The best return on your points is to use them for international business or first class flights with lie-flat seats. You would need 3 times more miles compared to an economy flight, but if you paid cash, you'd pay 5 - 10 times more than the cost of the economy flight, so it really pays to use your points only for upgrades. The worst value for your miles is to buy an economy seat or worse, a gift from the airlines gift-shop.

Sign up for a family/household account to pool miles together. If you share a common address, you can claim the miles with most airlines. You can use AwardWallet to keep track of your miles. Remember that they only last for 2 years, so use them before they expire.

How to get 70% off a Cruise

An average cruise can set you back $4,000. If you dream of cruising the oceans, but find the pricing too high, look at repositioning cruises. You can save as much as 70% by taking a cruise which takes the boat back to its home port.

These one-way itineraries take place during low cruise seasons when ships have to reposition themselves to locations where there's warmer weather.

To find a repositioning cruise, go to vacationstogo.com/repositioning_cruises.cfm. This simple and often overlooked booking trick is great for avoiding long flights with children and can save you so much money!

It's worth noting we don't have any affiliations with any travel service or provider. The links we suggest are chosen based on our experience of finding the best deals.

Relaxing at the Airport

The best way to relax at the airport is in a lounge where they provide free food, drinks, comfortable chairs, luxurious amenities (many have showers) and, if you're lucky, a peaceful ambience. If you're there for a longer time, look for Airport Cubicles, sleep pods which charge by the hour.

You can use your FFP Card (Frequent Flyer Memberships) to get into select lounges for free. Check your eligibility before you pay.

If you're travelling a lot, I'd recommend investing in a Priority Pass for the airport.

It includes 850-plus airport lounges around the world. The cost is $99 for the year and $27 per lounge visit or you can pay $399 for the year all inclusive.

If you need a lounge for a one-off day, you can get a Day Pass. Buy it online for a discount, it always works out cheaper than buying at the airport. Use www.LoungePass.com.

Lounges are also great if you're travelling with kids, as they're normally free for kids and will definitely cost you less than snacks for your little ones. The rule is that kids should be seen and not heard, so consider this before taking an overly excited child who wants to run around, or you might be asked to leave even after you've paid.

How to spend money

Bank ATM fees vary from $2.50 per transaction to as high as $5 or more, depending on the ATM and the country. You can completely skip those fees by paying with card and using a card which can hold multiple currencies.

Budget travel hacking begins with a strategy to spend without fees. Your individual strategy depends on the country you legally reside in as to what cards are available. Happily there are some fin-tech solutions which can save you thousands on those pesky ATM withdrawal fees and are widely available globally. Here are a selection of cards you can pre-charge with currency for Fiji:

N26

N26 is a 12-year-old digital bank. I have been using them for over 6 years. The key advantage is fee-free card transactions abroad. They have a very elegant app, where you can check your timeline for all transactions listed in real time or manage your in-app security anywhere. The card you receive is a Mastercard so you can use it everywhere. If you lose the card, you don't have to call anyone, just open the app and swipe 'lock card'. It puts your purchases into a graph automatically so you can see what you spend on. You can open an account from abroad entirely online, all you need is your passport and a camera n26.com

Revolut

Revolut is a multi-currency account that allows you to hold and exchange 29 currencies and spend fee-free abroad. It's a UK based neobank, but accepts customers from all over the world.

Wise debit card

If you're going to be in one place for a long time, the Wise debit card is like having your travel money on a card – it lets you spend money at the real exchange rate.

Monzo

Monzo is good if your UK based. They offer a fee-free UK account. Fee-free international money transfers and fee-free spending abroad.

The downside

The cards above are debit cards, meaning you need to have money in those accounts to spend it. This comes with one big downside: safety. Credit card issuers' have "zero liability" meaning you're not liable for unauthorised charges. All the cards listed above do provide cover for unauthorised charges but times vary greatly in how quickly you'd get your money back if it were stolen.

The best option is to check in your country to see which credit cards are the best for travelling and set up monthly payments to repay the whole amount so you don't pay unnecessary interest. In the USA, Schwab regularly ranks at the top for travel credit cards. Credit cards are always the safer option when abroad simply because you get your money back faster if its stolen and if you're renting cars, most will give you free insurance when you book the car rental using the card, saving you money.

Always withdraw money; never exchange.

Money exchanges, whether they be on the streets or in the airports will NEVER give you a good exchange rate. Do not bring bundles of cash. Instead, withdraw local currency from the ATM as needed and try to use only free ATMs. Many in airports charge you a fee to withdraw cash. Look for bigger ATMs attached to banks to avoid this.

Recap

- Take cash from local, non-charging ATMs for the best rates.
- Never change at airport exchange desks unless you absolutely have to, then just change just enough to be able get to a bank ATM.
- Bring a spare credit card for emergencies.
- Split cash in various places on your person (pockets, shoes) and in your luggage. It's never sensible to keep your cash or cards all in one place.
- In higher risk areas, use a money belt under your clothes or put $50 in your shoe or bra.

Revolut
Revolut is a multi-currency account that allows you to hold and exchange 29 currencies and spend fee-free abroad. It's a UK based neobank, but accepts customers from all over the world.

Wise debit card
If you're going to be in one place for a long time the Wise debit card is like having your travel money on a card – it lets you spend money at the real exchange rate.

Monzo
Monzo is good if your UK based. They offer a fee-free UK account. Fee-free international money transfers and fee-free spending abroad.

The downside

The cards above are debit cards, meaning you need to have money in those accounts to spend it. This comes with one big downside: safety. Credit card issuers' have "zero liability" meaning you're not liable for unauthorised charges. All of the cards listed above do provide cover for unauthorised charges but times vary greatly in how quickly you'd get your money back if it were stolen.

The best option is to check in your country to see which credit cards are the best for travelling and set up monthly payments to repay the whole amount so you don't pay unnecessary interest. In the USA, Schwab[4] regularly ranks at the top for travel credit cards. Credit cards are always the safer option when abroad simply because you get your money back faster if its stolen and if you're renting cars, most will give you free insurance when you book the car rental using the card, saving you money.

Always withdraw money; never exchange.

Money exchanges whether they be on the streets or in the airports will NEVER give you a good exchange rate. Do not bring bundles of cash. Instead withdraw local currency from the ATM as needed and try to use only free ATM's. Many in airports charge you a fee to withdraw cash. Look for bigger ATM's attached to banks to avoid this.

Recap

- Take cash from local, non-charging ATMs for the best rates.
- Never change at airport exchange desks unless you absolutely have to, then just change just enough to be able get to a bank ATM.
- Bring a spare credit card for emergencies.
- Split cash in various places on your person (pockets, shoes) and in your luggage. Its never sensible to keep your cash or cards all in one place.
- In higher risk areas, use a money belt under your clothes or put $50 in your shoe or bra.

[4] Charles Schwab High Yield Checking accounts refund every single ATM fee worldwide, require no minimum balance and have no monthly fee.

How NOT to be ripped off

"One of the great things about travel is that you find out how many good, kind people ther e are."
— Edith Wharton

The quote above may seem ill placed in a chapter entitled how not to be ripped off, but I included it to remind you that the vast majority of people do not want to rip you off. In fact, scammers are normally limited to three situations:

1. Around heavily visited attractions - these places are targeted purposively due to sheer footfall. Many criminals believe ripping people off is simply a numbers game.

2. In cities or countries with low-salaries or communist ideologies. If they can't make money in the country, they seek to scam foreigners. If you have travelled to India, Morocco or Cuba you will have observed this phenomenon.

3. When you are stuck and the person helping you know you have limited options.

Scammers know that most people will avoid confrontation. Don't feel bad about utterly ignoring someone and saying no. Here are six strategies to avoid being ripped off:

1. **Never ever agree to pay as much as you want. Always decide on a price before.**

Whoever you're dealing with is trained to tell you, they are uninterested in money. This is a trap. If you let people do this they will ask for MUCH MORE money at the end, and because you have used there service, you will feel obliged to pay. This is a conman's trick and nothing more.

2. Pack light

You can move faster and easier. If you take heavy luggage, you will end up taking taxis which are comparatively very costly over time.

3. NEVER use the airport taxi service. Plan to use public transport before you reach the airport.

4. Don't buy a sim card from the airport. Buy from the local supermarkets it will cost 50% less.

5. Eat at local restaurants serving regional food

Food defines culture. Exploring all delights available to the palate doesn't need to cost enormous sums.

6. **Ask the locals what something should cost,** and try not to pay over that.

7. **If you find yourself with limited options.** e.g. your taxi dumps you on the side of the road because you refuse to pay more (common in India and parts of South America) don't act desperate and negotiate as if you have other options or you will be extorted.

8. Don't blindly rely on social media[5]

Let's say you post in a Facebook group that you want tips for travelling to The Maldives. A lot of the comments you will receive come from guides, hosts and restaurants doing their own promotion. It's estimated that 50% or more of Facebook's current monthly active users are fake. And what's worse, a recent study found Social media platforms leave 95% of reported fake accounts up. These accounts are the digital versions of the men who hang around the Grand Palace in Bangkok telling tourists its closed, to divert you to shops where they will receive a commission for bringing you.

It can also be the case that genuine comments come from people who have totally different interests, beliefs and yes, budgets to yours. Make your experience your own and don't believe every comment you read.

Bottom line: use caution when accepting recommendations on social media and always fact-check with your own research.

Small tweaks on the road add up to big differences in your bank balance

Take advantage of other hotel amenities

If you fancy a swim but you're nowhere near the ocean, try the nearest hotel with a pool. As long as you buy a drink, the hotel staff will probably grant you access.

Fill up your mini bar for free.

Fill up your mini bar for free by storing things from the breakfast bar or grocery shop in your mini bar to give you a greater selection of drinks and food without the hefty price tag.

Save yourself some ironing

Use the steam from the shower to get rid of wrinkles in clothing. If something is creased, leave it trapped with the steam in the bathroom overnight for even better results.

See somewhere else for free

Opt for long stopovers, allowing you to experience another city without spending much money.

Wear your heaviest clothes

On the plane to save weight in your pack, allowing you to bring more with you. Big coats can then be used as pillows to make your flight more comfortable.

Don't get lost while you're away.

Find where you want to go using Google Maps, then type 'OK Maps' into the search bar to store this information for offline viewing.

---

[5] https://arstechnica.com/tech-policy/2019/12/social-media-platforms-leave-95-of-reported-fake-accounts-up-study-finds/

Use car renting services

Share Now or Car2Go allow you to hire a car for 2 hours for $25 in a lot of European countries.

Share Rides

Use sites like blablacar.com to find others who are driving in your direction. It can be 80% cheaper than normal transport. Just check the drivers reviews.

Use free gym passes

Get a free gym day pass by googling the name of a local gym and free day pass.

When asked by people providing you a service where you are from..

If there's no price list for the service you are asking for, when asked where you are from, Say you are from a lesser-known poorer country. I normally say Macedonia, and if they don't know where it is, add it's a poor country. If you say UK, USA, the majority of Europe bar the well-known poorer countries taxi drivers, tour operators etc will match the price to what they think you pay at home.

Set-up a New Uber/ other car hailing app account for discounts

By googling you can find offers with $50 free for new users in most cities for Uber/ Lyft/ Bolt and alike. Just set up a new gmail.com email account to take advantage.

Where and How to Make Friends

"People don't take trips, trips take people." – John Steinbeck

Become popular at the airport

Want to become popular at the airport? Pack a power bar with multiple outlets and just see how many friends you can make. It's amazing how many people forget their chargers, or who packed them in the luggage that they checked in.

Stay in Hostels

First of all, Hostels don't have to be shared dorms, and they cater to a much wider demographic than is assumed. Hostels are a better environment for meeting people than hotels, and more importantly, they tended to open up excursion opportunities that further opened up that opportunity.

Or take up a hobby

If hostels are a definite no-no for you; find an interest. Take up a hobby where you will meet people. I've dived for years and the nature of diving is you're always paired up with a dive buddy. I met a lot of interesting people that way.

Small tweaks on the road add up to big differences in your bank balance

Take advantage of other hotel's amenities

If you fancy a swim but you're nowhere near the ocean, try the nearest hotel with a pool. As long as you buy a drink, the hotel staff will likely grant you access.

Fill up your mini bar for free.

Fill up your mini bar for free by storing things from the breakfast bar or grocery shop in your mini bar to give you a greater selection of drinks and food without the hefty price tag.

Save yourself some ironing

Use the steam from the shower to get rid of wrinkles in clothing. If something is creased, leave it trapped with the steam in the bathroom overnight for even better results.

See somewhere else for free

Opt for long stopovers, allowing you to experience another city without spending much money.

Wear your heaviest clothes

on the plane to save weight in your pack, allowing you to bring more with you. Big coats can then be used as pillows to make your flight more comfortable.

Don't get lost while you're away.

Find where you want to go using Google Maps, then type 'OK Maps' into the search bar to store this information for offline viewing.

Use car renting services

Share Now or Car2Go allow you to hire a car for 2 hours for $25 in a lot of Europe.

Share Rides

Use sites like blablacar.com to find others who are driving in your direction. It can be 80% cheaper than normal transport. Just check the drivers reviews.

Use free gym passes

Get a free gym day pass by googling the name of a local gym and free day pass.

When asked by people providing you a service where you are from..

If there's no price list for the service you are asking for, when asked where you are from, Say you are from a lesser-known poorer country. I normally say Macedonia, and if they don't know where it is, add it's a poor country. If you say UK, USA, the majority of Europe bar the well-known poorer countries taxi drivers, tour operators etc will match the price to what they think you pay at home.

Set-up a New Uber/ other car hailing app account for discounts

By googling you can find offers with $50 free for new users in most cities for Uber/ Lyft/ Bolt and alike. Just set up a new gmail.com email account to take advantage.

Where and How to Make Friends

"People don't take trips, trips take people." – John Steinbeck

Become popular at the airport

Want to become popular at the airport? Pack a power bar with multiple outlets and just see how many friends you can make. It's amazing how many people forget their chargers, or who packed them in the luggage that they checked in.

Stay in Hostels

First of all, Hostels don't have to be shared dorms, and they cater to a much wider demographic than is assumed. Hostels are a better environment for meeting people than hotels, and more importantly they tended to open up excursion opportunities that further opened up that opportunity.

Or take up a hobby

If hostels are a definite no-no for you; find an interest. Take up a hobby where you will meet people. I've dived for years and the nature of diving is you're always paired up with a dive buddy. I met a lot of interesting people that way.

When unpleasantries come your way...

We all have our good and bad days travelling, and on a bad day you can feel like just taking a flight home. Here are some ways to overcome common travel problems:

Anxiety when flying

It has been over 40 years since a plane has been brought down by turbulence. Repeat that number to yourself: 40 years! Planes are built to withstand lighting strikes, extreme storms and ultimately can adjust course to get out of their way. Landing and take-off are when the most accidents happen, but you have statistically three times the chance of winning a huge jackpot lottery, then you do of dying in a plane crash.

If you feel afraid on the flight, focus on your breathing saying the word 'smooth' over and over until the flight is smooth. Always check the airline safety record on airlinerating.com I was surprised to learn Ryanair and Easyjet as much less safe than Wizz Air according to those ratings because they sell similarly priced flights. If there is extreme turbulence, I feel much better knowing I'm in a 7 star safety plane.

Wanting to sleep instead of seeing new places

This is a common problem. Just relax, there's little point doing fun things when you feel tired. Factor in jet-lag to your travel plans. When you're rested and alert you'll enjoy your new temporary home much more. Many people hate the first week of a long-trip because of jet-lag and often blame this on their first destination, but its rarely true. Ask travellers who 'hate' a particular place and you will see that very often they either had jet-lag or an unpleasant journey there.

Going over budget

Come back from a trip to a monster credit card bill? Hopefully, this guide has prevented you from returning to an unwanted bill. Of course, there are costs that can creep up and this is a reminder about how to prevent them making their way on to your credit card bill:

- To and from the airport. Solution: leave adequate time and take the cheapest method - book before.
- Baggage. Solution: take hand luggage and post things you might need to yourself.
- Eating out. Solution: go to cheap eats places and suggest those to friends.
- Parking. Solution: use apps to find free parking
- Tipping. Solution Leave a modest tip and tell the server you will write them a nice review.
- Souvenirs. Solution: fridge magnets only.

- Giving to the poor. (This one still gets me, but if you're giving away $10 a day - it adds up) Solution: volunteer your time instead and recognise that in tourist destinations many beggars are run by organised crime gangs.

Price v Comfort

I love traveling. I don't love struggling. I like decent accommodation, being able to eat properly and see places and enjoy. I am never in the mood for low-cost airlines or crappy transfers, so here's what I do to save money.

- Avoid organised tours unless you are going to a place where safety is a real issue. They are expensive and constrain your wanderlust to typical things. I only recommend them in Algeria, Iran and Papua New Guinea - where language and gender views pose serious problems all cured by a reputable tour organiser.
- Eat what the locals do.
- Cook in your Airbnb/ hostel where restaurants are expensive.
- Shop at local markets.
- Spend time choosing your flight, and check the operator on arilineratings.com
- Mix up hostels and Airbnbs. Hostels for meeting people, Airbnb for relaxing and feeling 'at home'.

Not knowing where free toilets are

Use Toilet Finder - https://play.google.com/store/apps/details?id=com.bto.toilet&hl=en

Your Airbnb is awful

Airbnb customer service is notoriously bad. Help yourself out. Try to sort things out with the host, but if you can't, take photos of everything e.g bed, bathroom, mess, doors, contact them within 24 hours. Tell them you had to leave and pay for new accommodation. Ask politely for a full refund including booking fees. With photographic evidence and your new accommodation receipt, they can't refuse.

The airline loses your bag

Go to the Luggage desk before leaving the airport and report the bag missing. Hopefully you've headed the advice to put an AirTag in your checked bag and you can show them where to find your bag. Most airlines will give you an overnight bag, ask where you're staying and return the bag to you within three days. It's extremely rare for Airlines to lose your bag due to technological innovation, but if that happens you should submit an insurance claim after the three days is up, including receipts for everything you had to buy in the interim.

Your travel companion lets you down

Whether it's a breakup or a friend cancelling, it sucks and can ramp up costs. The easiest solution to finding a new travel companion is to go to a well-reviewed hostel and find someone you want to travel with. You should spend at least three days getting to know this person before you suggest travelling together. Finding someone in person is always better than finding someone online, because you can get a better idea of whether you will have a smooth journey together. Travel can make or break friendships.

Culture shock

I had one of the strongest culture shocks while spending 6 months in Japan. It was overwhelming how much I had to prepare when I went outside of the door (googling words and sentences what to use, where to go, which station and train line to use, what is this food called in Japanese and how does its look etc.). I was so tired constantly but in the end I just let go and went with my extremely bad Japanese. If you feel culture shocked its because your brain is referencing your surroundings to what you know. Stop comparing, have Google translate downloaded and relax.

Your Car rental insurance is crazy expensive

I always use carrentals.com and book with a credit card. Most credit cards will give you free insurance for the car, so you don't need to pay the extra. Some unsavoury companies will bump the price up when you arrive. Ask to speak to a manager. If this doesn't resolve, it google "consumer ombudsman for NAME OF COUNTRY." and seek an immediate full refund on the balance difference you paid. It is illegal in most countries to alter the price of a rental car when the person arrives to pickup a pre-arranged car.

A note on Car Rental Insurance

Always always always rent a car with a credit card that has rental vehicle coverage built into the card and is automatically applied when you rent a car. Then there's no need to buy additional rental insurance (check with your card on the coverage they protect some exclude collision coverage). Do yourself a favour when you step up to the desk to rent the car tell the agent you're already covered and won't be buying anything today. They work on commission and you'll save time and your patience avoiding the upselling.

You're sick

First off ALWAYS, purchase travel insurance. Including emergency transport up to $500k even to back home, which is usually less than $10 additional. I use https://www.comparethemarket.com/travel-insurance/ to find the best days. If I am sick I normally check into a hotel with room service and ride it out.

Make a Medication Travel Kit

Take travel sized medications with you:

- Antidiarrheal medication (for example, bismuth subsalicylate, loperamide)
- Medicine for pain or fever (such as acetaminophen, aspirin, or ibuprofen)
- Throat Lozenges

Save yourself from most travel related hassles

- Do not make jokes with immigration and customs staff. A misunderstanding can lead to HUGE fines.
- Book the most direct flight you can find nonstop if possible.
- Carry a US$50 bill for emergency cash. I have entered a country and all ATM and credit card systems were down. US$ can be exchanged nearly anywhere in the world and is useful in extreme situations, but where possible don't exchange, as you will lose money.
- Check, and recheck, required visas and such BEFORE the day of your trip. Some countries, for instance, require a ticket out of the country in order to enter. Others, like the US and Australia, require electronic authorisation in advance.
- Airport security is asinine and inconsistent around the world. Keep this in mind when connecting flights. Always leave at least 2 hours for international connections or international to domestic. In Stansted for example, they force you to buy one of their plastic bags, and remove your liquids from your own plastic bag.... just to make money from you. And this adds to the time it will take to get through security, so lines are long.
- Wiki travel is perfect to use for a lay of the land.
- Expensive luggage rarely lasts longer than cheap luggage, in my experience. Fancy leather bags are toast with air travel.

Food

- When it comes to food, eat in local restaurants, not tourist-geared joints. Any place with the menu in three or more languages is going to be overpriced.
- Take a spork - a knife, spoon and fork all in one.

Water Bottle

Take a water bottle with a filter. We love these ones from Water to Go.

Empty it before airport security and separate the bottle and filter as some airport people will try and claim it has liquids...

Bug Sprays

If you're heading somewhere tropical spray your clothes with Permethrin before you travel. It lasts 40 washes and saves space in your bag. A 'Bite Away' zapper can be used after the bite to totally erase it. It cuts down on the itching and erases the bite from your skin.

Order free mini's

Don't buy those expensive travel sized toiletries, order travel sized freebies online. This gives you the opportunity to try brands you've never used before, and who knows, you might even find your new favourite soap.

Take a waterproof bag

If you're travelling alone you can swim without worrying about your phone, wallet and passport laying on the beach.

You can also use it as a source of entertainment on those ultra budget flights.

Make a private entertainment centre anywhere

Always take an eye-mask, earplugs, a scarf and a kindle reader - so you can sleep and entertain yourself anywhere!

The best Travel Gadgets

The door alarm

If you're nervous and staying in private rooms or airbnbs take a door alarm. For those times when you just don't feel safe, it can help you fall asleep. You can get tiny ones for less than $10 from Online Retailers: https://www.Online Retailers.com/Travel-door-alarm/s?k=Travel+door+alarm

Smart Blanket

Online Retailers sells a 6 in 1 heating blanket that is very useful for cold plane or bus trips. Its great if you have poor circulation as it becomes a detachable Foot Warmer: Online Retailers http://amzn.to/2hTYIOP I paid $49.00.

The coat that becomes a tent

https://www.adiff.com/products/tent-jacket. This is great if you're going to be doing a lot of camping.

Clever Tank Top with Secret Pockets

Keep your valuables safe in this top. Perfect for all climates.

on Online

Retailers for $39.90

Optical Camera Lens for Smartphones and Tablets

Leave your bulky camera at home. Turn your device into a high-performance camera. Buy on Online Retailers for $9.95

Travel-sized Wireless Router with USB Media Storage

Convert any wired network to a wireless network. Buy on Online Retailers for $17.99

Buy a Scrubba Bag to wash your clothes on the go

Or a cheaper imitable. You can wash your clothes on the go.

Hacks for Families

Rent an Airbnb apartment so you can cook

Apartments are much better for families, as you have all the amenities you'd have at home. They are normally cheaper per person too. We are the first travel guide publisher to include Airbnb's in our recommendations if you think any of these need updating you can email me at philgtang@gmail.com

Shop at local markets

Eat seasonal products and local products. Get closer to the local market and observe the prices and the offer. What you can find more easily, will be the cheapest.

Take Free Tours

Download free podcast tours of the destination you are visiting. The podcast will tell you where to start, where to go, and what to look for. Often you can find multiple podcast tours of the same place. Listen to all of them if you like, each one will tell you a little something new.

Pack Extra Ear Phones

If you go on a museum tour, they often have audio guides. Instead of having to rent one for each person, take some extra earphones. Most audio tour devices have a place to plug in a second set.

Buy Souvenirs Ahead of Time

If you are buying souvenirs somewhere touristy, you are paying a premium price. By ordering the same exact products online, you can save a lot of money.

Use Cheap Transportation

Do as the locals do, including weekly passes.

Carry Reusable Water Bottles

Spending money on water and other beverages can quickly add up. Instead of paying for drinks, take some refillable water bottles.

Combine Attractions

Many major cities offer ticket bundles where one price gets you into 5 or 6 popular attractions. You will need to plan ahead of time to decide what things you plan to do on vacation and see if they are selling these activities together.

Pack Snacks

Granola bars, apples, baby carrots, bananas, cheese crackers, juice boxes, pretzels, fruit snacks, apple sauce, grapes, and veggie chips.

Stick to Carry-On Bags

Do not pay to check a large bag. Even a small child can pull a carry-on.

Visit free art galleries and museums

Just google the name + free days.

Eat Street Food

There's a lot of unnecessary fear around this. You can watch the food prepared. Go for the stands that have a steady queue.

Travel Gadgets for Families

Dropcam

Are what-if scenarios playing out in your head? Then you need Dropcam.

'Dropcam HD Internet Wi-Fi Video Monitoring Cameras help you watch what you love from anywhere. In less than a minute, you'll have it setup and securely streaming video to you over your home Wi-Fi. Watch what you love while away with Dropcam HD.'

Approximate Price: $139

Kelty-Child-Carrier

Voted as one of the best hiking essentials if you're traveling with kids and can carry a child up to 18kg.

Jetkids Bedbox

No more giving up your own personal space on the plane with this suitcase that becomes a bed.

How I got hooked on luxury on a budget travelling

'We're on holiday' is what my dad used to say to justify getting us in so much debt we lost our home and all our things when I was 11. We moved from the suburban bliss of Hemel Hempstead to a run down council estate in inner-city London, near my dad's new job as a refuge collector, a fancy word for dustbin man. I lost all my school friends while watching my dad go through a nervous breakdown.

My dad loved walking up a hotel lobby desk without a care in the world. So much so, that he booked overpriced holidays on credit cards. A lot of holidays. As it turned out, we couldn't afford any of them. In the end, my dad had no choice but to declare bankruptcy. When my mum realised, he'd racked up so much debt our family unit dissolved. A neat and perhaps as painless a summary of events that lead me to my life's passion: budget travel that doesn't compromise on fun, safety or comfort.

I started travelling full-time at the age of 18. I wrote the first Super Cheap Insider guide for friends visiting Norway - which I did for a month on less than $250. When sales reached 10,000 I decided to form the Super Cheap Insider Guides company. As I know from first-hand experience debt can be a noose around our necks, and saying 'oh come on, we're on vacation' isn't a get out of jail free card. In fact, its the reverse of what travel is supposed to bring you - freedom.

Before I embarked upon writing Super Cheap Insider guides, many, many people told me that my dream was impossible. Travelling on a budget could never be comfortable. I hope this guide has proved to you what I have known for a long-time: budget travel can feel luxurious when you know and use the insider hacks.

And apologies if I depressed you with my tale of woe. My dad is now happily remarried and works as a chef in Fiji at a fancy hotel - the kind he used to take us to!

A final word...

There's a simple system you can use to think about budget travel. In life, we can choose two of the following: cheap, fast, or quality. So if you want it Cheap and fast you will get a lower quality service. Fast-food is the perfect example. The system holds true for purchasing anything while travelling. I always choose cheap and quality, except at times where I am really limited on time. Normally, you can make small tweaks to make this work for you. Ultimately, you must make choices about what's most important to you and heed your heart's desires.

'Your heart is the most powerful muscle in your body. Do what it says.' Jen Sincero

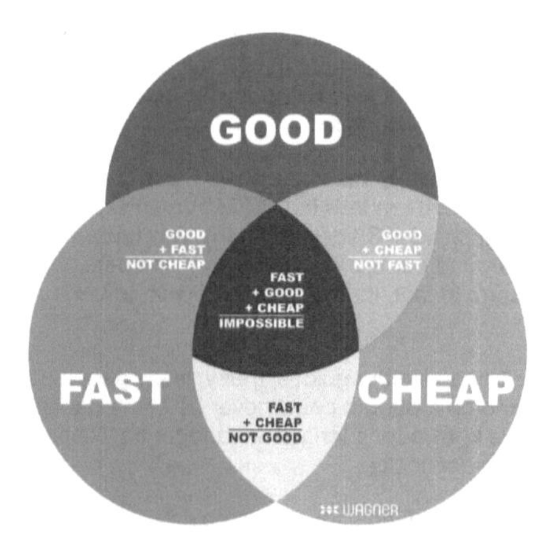

If you've found this book useful, please select some stars, it would mean genuinely make my day to see I've helped you.

Copyright

Published in Great Britain in 2024 by Super Cheap Insider Guides LTD.

Made in United States
Troutdale, OR
12/27/2024